SEATTLE
STAIRWAY WALKS

SEATTLE
STAIRWAY WALKS

An Up-and-Down Guide to City Neighborhoods

Jake Jaramillo &
Cathy Jaramillo

THE MOUNTAINEERS BOOKS

৵

To Norman and Sheila,
with whom we spent many hours of happy discovery
along the stairways of Los Angeles;
and Adah Bakalinsky, who wrote the book.

The Mountaineers Books
is the nonprofit publishing arm of The Mountaineers,
an organization founded in 1906 and dedicated to the exploration,
preservation, and enjoyment of outdoor and wilderness areas.

1001 SW Klickitat Way, Suite 201, Seattle, WA 98134

© 2013 by Jake Jaramillo and Cathy Jaramillo

First edition: first printing 2013, second printing 2013

Manufactured in China

Copy Editor: Jane Crosen
Cover and Book Design: Peggy Egerdahl
Cartographer: Pease Press Cartography
All photographs by Cathy Jaramillo unless otherwise noted.

Cover photograph: *The 38th Avenue stairs in Madrona*
Frontispiece: *The Galer stairs from Queen Anne Boulevard*

Library of Congress Cataloging-in-Publication Data
Jaramillo, Jake.
  Seattle stairway walks : an up-and-down guide to city neighborhoods / by Jake and
Cathy Jaramillo.
    p. cm.
  Includes index.
  ISBN 978-1-59485-677-8 (pbk) — ISBN 978-1-59485-678-5 (ebook)
  1. Seattle (Wash.)—Tours. 2. Walking—Washington (State)—Seattle—Guidebooks.
3. Stairs—Washington (State)—Seattle—Guidebooks. I. Jaramillo, Cathy. II. Title.
  F869.S5945J37 2012
  917.97'77204—dc23
                          2012018924

ISBN (paperback): 978-159485-677-8
ISBN (ebook): 978-59485-678-5

CONTENTS

LEGEND

——— Route on Street	▬▬▬ Street	
▪▪▪▪▪▪ Route on Stairway	▬▬▬ Major Street	
------ Featured Path	▬▬▬ Highway	
——— Optional Street	▬▬▬ Freeway	
▪▪▪▪▪▪ Optional Stairs	⑤ Interstate Highway	
------ Optional Path	㊙ State Highway	
▪▪▪▪▪▪ Other Stairway	**S** Start/Finish	
------ Other Path	**F** Separate Finish	
Puget Water	⊕ Restrooms	
Cedar Park	卅 Picnic Area	
Other Public Land	᐀ Bridge	
Large Building	• Point of Interest	
	1 Numbered Directions	

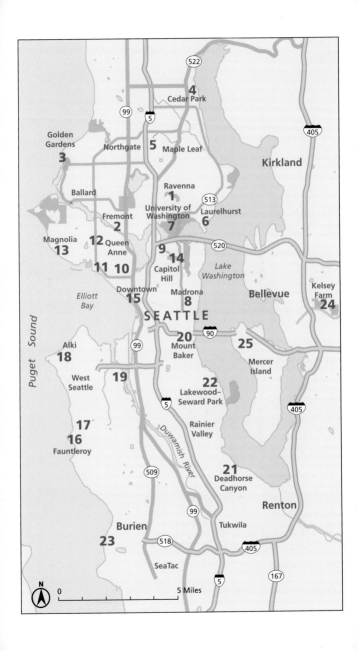

SEATTLE STAIRWAY WALKS BY MILEAGE WITH STEPS

WALK NUMBER/NAME	MILES	STEPS DOWN	STEPS UP
23. Burien: Eagle Landing Stairs	0.4	289	289
17. Solstice Park	1.0	70	0
24. Bellevue: Kelsey Creek Farm	1.2	50	163
3. Golden Gardens	1.4	272	272
1. Ravenna	1.6	118	264
8. Madrona and Leschi	1.7	371	299
19. Longfellow Creek and Pigeon Point	1.8	274	314
21. Deadhorse Canyon and Rainier Beach	1.8	307	120
22. Lakewood-Seward Park	1.8	174	207
6. Laurelhurst	1.9	222	101
25. Mercer Island: Mercerdale Hillside	2.0	522	329
9. Eastlake, North Capitol Hill, and Portage Bay	2.3	349	337
20. Mount Baker	2.4	569	372
15. Downtown: City Hall to Pike Place	2.5	385	455
7. University of Washington	2.6	273	325
11. Southwest Queen Anne	2.6	588	477
12. Northwest Queen Anne	3.0	308	216
2. Fremont	3.2	224	302
4. Cedar Park and the Burke-Gilman Trail	3.2	275	196
18. Alki From Above	3.4	374	73
16. Fauntleroy and Morgan Junction	3.5	495	69
10. East Queen Anne	3.7	300	501
14. The Olmsted Vision: The Arboretum, Interlaken Park, and Volunteer Park	4.2	243	359
13. South Magnolia	4.5	327	405
5. Maple Leaf and Thornton Creek	4.7	326	136

INTRODUCTION: SCENIC
BYWAYS OF THE CITY

Without doubt Seattle has some of the most complicated and beautiful urban topography in the country. First-time visitors are sometimes surprised by this, but most locals are used to living with natural barriers all around: hills, like Capitol Hill and Queen Anne; bluffs, like those overlooking Lake Washington and Puget Sound; canyons, like Ravenna Ravine and Deadhorse Canyon; and multiple bodies of water like Green Lake, Lake Union, and the Ship Canal.

This complicated topography gives Seattle a distinctive look and feel, and it also makes for lots of stairways, many of them constructed more than a century ago. Stairways used to perform a workaday function in neighborhoods all over town, getting people from house to trolley stop in the morning, and back at night. Since then they've become our neighborhood scenic byways, and this book is all about exploring them. On these stairway routes you'll find there isn't one "best view" in the city. You'll see great views and make new discoveries around every corner—maybe even your own!

It's fascinating how Seattle got to be like this. Long before there was a city here or anywhere else, this area was entombed under a three-thousand-foot-deep sheet of ice. It seems that massive continental ice flows came and went at least four times over a two-million-year period. The last episode left a deep impression as it retreated, fourteen thousand years ago, gouging and smashing and spitting out a jumbled landscape. The natural channels and barriers that were left behind have shaped our urban layout and deeply affect our experience in the city. This place feels physically intricate and intimate, full of nooks and crannies just waiting to be discovered.

Of course, cultural and historical factors played a big role, too. In 1853 the United States established the Northwest Territory, naming Isaac Stevens as first territorial governor. Stevens quickly went to work opening the territory to settlement and development. He used a variety of tactics, some underhanded, some violent, to push the area's first human inhabitants, the Puget Salish people, to reservations across the Sound. This left the field open for settlement, centered at first on logging and milling. Coal mining made a brief appearance on the east side of Lake Washington. Small, widely scattered, and hastily built hamlets sprang up around these operations—future nodes of a "city of neighborhoods."

By 1900 logging had mostly played out. Landowners realized that additional value might be extracted by creating residential developments on their freshly denuded tracts. Very often, the first step was to build a horse-drawn trolley or streetcar line out to some far-removed area, perhaps one of those pre-existing hamlets. This lured developers, who could then purchase the land, build homes, and sell them to new residents. The trolley stops became the natural commercial hubs of nascent neighborhoods, where folks could stop by a tavern, laundry, grocery, or hardware store on their last leg home from work. Many neighborhoods still have that "village hub" feel (Madrona, Madison Park, Loyal Heights, or West Seattle, for example).

Stairways were first built as a way for developers to expand and extend the links between these trolley stops and residential tracts. Sometimes stairways even linked two trolley lines—like the Howe stairs, which, at 388 steps, is the longest stairway in Seattle and the fourth-longest in the country. It was built in 1911 to tie one trolley line running along the top of Capitol Hill with another running along Eastlake.

Ultimately, Seattle ended up with as many as 650 publicly accessible stairways. San Francisco has a similar number, Pittsburgh is said to have 730, Cincinnati more than 400, and Portland, Oregon, more than 200. In each of these cities, stairways have moved on from their original purpose. They've become scenic byways in and between neighborhoods, and perfect places to exercise and socialize. Here, they provide constant discoveries of cool and surprising neighborhood features you probably wouldn't see otherwise: colorful mosaics that turn a house's retaining wall into folk art; the quiet pocket park with a killer view of Portage Bay; a recently daylighted and restored creek; gorgeous homes on a historic boulevard; a bustling neighborhood café. Just walk Seattle's stairways, and you're guaranteed moments of urban serendipity like these.

Stairway walking can carry you outdoors into the heart of urban nature all year long. Keep an eye out for blooms and critters, birds and plants. They're changing all the time, constantly remaking the look and feel of each neighborhood. If you happen to love trekking in the mountains, hiking Seattle's stairs is a fun way to stay in shape while local trails clear in spring. Of course stairway walking is good exercise any time, whatever your age, fitness level, or interest.

We hope you use this book throughout the year to explore the quirky, interesting, and beautiful stairways and neighborhoods of Seattle, in the good company of family and friends.

ACKNOWLEDGMENTS

Thanks to the many people who contributed to this book in a variety of ways, among them our "stairway aficionado" friends Doug Beyerlein, Melissa Cate Christ, Susan Gilmore, Troy Heerwagen, Thomas Horton, Susan Ott and Dave Ralph, Jack Tomkinson, and Linnea Westerlind. Lisa Quinn of Feet First helps promote stairway walks in Seattle; John Buswell, Ainalem Molla, and Greg Kim from Seattle Department of Transportation's (SDOT's) Roadway Structures Division cheerfully answered our questions about stairs. Thanks to Rachel Lawson and Joseph Brown, who showed us some of the byways of Queen Anne. Thanks to the anonymous woman we encountered cross-country skiing in Idaho, who told us about the fabulous Laurelcrest Lane stairs back home. A myriad of folks told us their stories, among them Dan Streissguth, Jeannie Hale, Liz Ogden, Ruth Williams, Peter Mason, Nannette Martin, Joyce Moty, Ed MacLeod, and Carla Mottola.

HOW TO USE THIS BOOK

Each chapter represents a different Seattle neighborhood and stairway route. At the beginning of each route you'll find an overview of that walk's main highlights and attractions. Then there are a few standard, key details for quick reference:

- ♦ Length: In miles; all walks are loops unless otherwise noted.
- ♦ Walking Time: The average time it takes an adult to do the walk at leisurely pace.
- ♦ Steps Down/Up: The number of stairway steps.
- ♦ Kid-Friendly: Whether the route is suitable for young children, and related notes.
- ♦ Cafes/Pubs: Recommended places to stop for a rest, snack, drink, or picnic.
- ♦ Getting There: Driving directions to the closest intersection near the start of the walk, and bus routes with stops nearby.

Route Description: Each stairway walk has full directions, described in route segments (example: "To the 52nd Street Stairs [218 steps up]..."). Each segment references a numbered site on the map (a destination, point of interest, junction, or other landmark), so you can match directions with places.

Maps: Follow the site number sequence and direction-of-travel arrows to see what direction the route takes. The general location of major stairways is shown, as are footbridges, restrooms, and the starting and ending points.

Route Options: Occasionally, supplemental routes (side trips from the main route or to nearby attractions) are provided for further exploration. In some cases we suggest a shorter, more kid-friendly option. As space allows, directions and maps are provided in the book, but in other cases we refer you to the book website. **WWW**

Safety Notes: Safety is our first consideration, so we try to alert you when the route crosses a street or a main arterial (streets with yellow lane markers) without a crosswalk, goes down a narrow lane, etc. Only you can keep yourself safe; keep alert near traffic and use caution at all times.

Quick Response (QR) Codes: At the end of each stairway walk, you'll notice a QR code like this:

If you have a smartphone, you can use the code to read abbreviated directions for each walk on your phone, as you go, rather than taking the book along. First you'll need to download a code reader. Search your phone's app store for "QR code reader" and you should find several to choose from.

Seattle Stairways Website: Visit for more photos or options for each walk, add your comments and questions, get news about group walks, etc. at www.seattlestairwaywalks.com.

Special Symbols: Occasionally you'll see special symbols in the text.

PARK This symbol shows up only in the table of contents. It identifies walks where you'll spend a predominant amount of time in parks or greenspaces, or where these spaces will significantly shape the walk experience.

WWW This symbol tells you whenever there's related content on the book website.

Change Happens. Things are always changing, all over the city. We can't guarantee that everything we mention will still be there by the time you get to it, or in the same condition. This is especially true of places we name where you can get a snack or something to drink. If that happens, we hope you'll discover something delightful in its place! Bus routes may change too, so it's always a good idea to check Metro Transit's Online Trip Planner; search online for "Metro KC Trip Planner."

PART I

NORTH SEATTLE

1 Ravenna

Ravenna, just north of the University of Washington, is a typically busy university neighborhood. Cars and bikes constantly ply the major streets, and pedestrians are out and about throughout the day. This stairway walk takes you away from all that, onto the side streets, up hillsides, and into the deep ravine at the quiet heart of this gorgeous neighborhood.

The route climbs four blocks up the 52nd Street stairs before gradually descending along quiet residential streets toward Ravenna Park. Here, you'll step down a timber stairway into the hushed depths of the ravine that lies at the core of the park and the surrounding neighborhood. You'll stroll alongside the recently daylighted Ravenna Creek, liberated from its conduit to flow freely aboveground, blossoming under the care of neighborhood volunteers. You'll also cross two of three footbridges that span various parts of the ravine. The largest of these, at NE 20th Street, provides lofty views up and down the ravine. An optional loop takes you along its entire 0.5-mile length, with attractive playgrounds and resting places at either end.

If you have time, explore the extra neighborhood attractions mentioned below. These include Ravenna Boulevard, created as part of John C. Olmsted's 1903 parks plan; "Professors Row" is a quiet, leafy stretch of Ravenna Boulevard edging the south side of the ravine. Lined with graceful, exceptionally well-tended homes, Professors Row feels like a time and place apart.

Length:	**1.6 miles (add 0.8 mile with optional Upper Ravenna Park loop)**
Walking Time:	1 hour 15 minutes (add 30 minutes with optional Upper Ravenna Park loop)
Steps Down:	118
Steps Up:	264
Kid-Friendly:	The steps at the beginning might be too much for small children, but the ravine portion is a great little nature walk, with play areas on both ends.

Cafes/Pubs: Look along 25th Avenue NE, between NE 55th Street and University Village at the south end, or in University Village itself. For more of a neighborhood experience, try Cowen Park Grocery, which has great cafe/lunch fare. It's near the west end of Ravenna/Cowen parks, at Brooklyn Avenue NE and NE Ravenna Boulevard.

Getting There: If driving, park on NE 55th Street, at the southeast side of Ravenna Park right alongside the ballfield, which also marks the end of the route. Several bus routes stop at the corner of 25th Avenue NE and NE 55th Street, near the starting point: Metro Transit Route 30 from Sand Point; MT 74 from Downtown; MT 243 from Jackson Park; MT 68 from Northgate; and MT 243 from Bellevue.

To the 52nd Street Stairs (218 steps up): From the north side of NE 55th Street, carefully cross south toward Ravenna Avenue NE (not Ravenna Place). Traffic can come fast from several directions here, so be alert and use the crosswalks! Continue south on Ravenna Avenue, passing NE 53rd Street on your left. About a half block beyond 53rd, look for a short flight of stairs on the

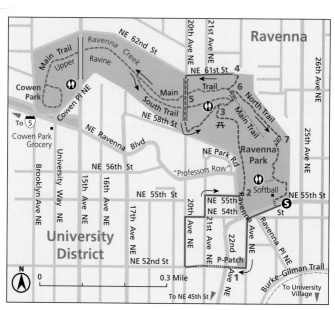

Down Ravenna Ravine

west side of the street. WWW It leads to a pathway going back from the street and past a P-Patch garden on the right. At the back of the P-Patch you'll find the base of the 52nd Street stairs (1).

At the top of the first flight, cross 22nd Avenue to reach the second flight, which has a small plaque at the base commemorating Seattle Department of Transportation's (SDOT's) rehabilitation of these stairs via the "Bridging the Gap" bond program. Midway up the second flight on the left side of the stairs, a small house nestles among cedars and below a large stand of bamboo, giving it a sort of treehouse effect. WWW

Cross 21st Avenue NE to begin the third and final flight. At the top, continue up a short cul-de-sac to 20th Avenue NE and turn right. Walk one block, then turn right again onto NE 54th Street. After one block on NE 54th, turn left onto 21st Avenue NE. Walk just one block, then turn right onto NE 55th Street. Continue ahead one block to cross Ravenna Avenue NE and head into Ravenna Park (2).

EVOLUTION OF RAVENNA RAVINE

According to geologists, the Seattle area has been buried under ice thousands of feet deep at least four times in the last two million years. The last ice sheet left behind a complicated network of hills and valleys, one of which became the basin for what we know as Green Lake. For centuries, water in this basin flowed east near the route of Ravenna Boulevard, slowly carving out Ravenna Ravine.

The town of Ravenna was annexed to Seattle in 1907, at the same time as West Seattle, Ballard, Southeast Seattle, South Park, and Columbia City. These annexations almost doubled the city's territory during a time of remarkable growth. Development ultimately cut off the Green Lake drainage, leaving Ravenna Creek to be fed solely by springs along the ravine.

The developer who platted Ravenna, W. W. Beck, owned and ran the ravine as a pay-to-enter attraction until he sold it to Seattle Parks and Recreation in 1911. The few remaining old-growth trees in the ravine were cut down soon after. In the 1960s much of the ravine at the upstream (northwest) end was filled in with debris from the construction of I-5, and the Cowen Park playground and meadow were built on top of it. At the lower end, Ravenna Creek was drained via pipeline into the sewer system.

In 1990, the city proposed to divert Ravenna Creek away from the sewer system and send it into Union Bay. A neighborhood coalition counterproposed a larger project, in which Ravenna Creek would be daylighted (i.e., restored from a pipeline to an aboveground channel) throughout the ravine all the way to Union Bay. Local merchants, including the owners of University Village, objected to this vision, so a compromise plan was adopted, in which Ravenna Creek would be daylighted only along the length of the ravine, then drained out of the lower ravine through a dedicated pipeline into Union Bay (see "Down the Drain").

From Ravenna Park Entrance to the Ravine: After entering the park, walk up the gravel trail for a few yards, turning left onto a larger path. You'll see restrooms on the right, just beyond a small play area with rope ladders, slides, and swings. Continue up the path past the tennis courts, also on the right. You'll enter a grove of second-growth maple, cedar, and madrona trees, as the path begins to angle uphill and to the left.

As the path straightens, you'll see a log fence on the right and a broad grassy area with a picnic shelter on the left. **WWW** The fence marks the south lip of Ravenna Ravine. Before reaching the restrooms ahead, look for a wooden sign on the right across the grass at the edge of the ravine. About 10 yards to the right of the sign you'll find the top of your next stairway (3), leading down into the ravine. Ignore the trail next to the sign, and take the stairs down.

Ravenna Ravine Stairway to Side Ravine (18 steps up, 59 steps down): There are several landings along this stairway where you can take stock of the view. In winter you might be able to glimpse a footbridge across the ravine, through the bare trees. Soon enough, you'll be walking on it! `WWW`

At the base of the stairs, continue down the path, interrupted by 18 scattered steps on the way to the bottom of the ravine. Curve left toward a small footbridge across Ravenna Creek, ignoring side paths. Cross the bridge, taking note of this spot, which you'll encounter again. After crossing Ravenna Creek, you'll be heading toward the west end of the ravine, along the main walkway.

Just after the bridge, you'll pass a small pathway on the right heading up the ravine, marked by a sign for "RAVENNA PARK TRAIL SYSTEM NE 58TH STREET." You'll take this trail later, but for now continue another 5 yards down the main path, where you'll encounter a lovely little tributary to Ravenna Creek flowing down a side ravine from the right.

About 15 feet beyond this tributary, turn right onto a side trail marked by a couple of timber steps leading uphill, signed "RAVENNA PARK TRAIL SYSTEM NE 62ND STREET." Climb the steps and continue straight up this trail, past smaller trails on either side. You'll climb 18 more pathway steps before arriving at another footbridge (4).

Side Ravine and Main Ravine Footbridges (28 steps up): At the top of the trail, turn left to cross the footbridge over a side ravine. Just behind you, out of sight, is a second bridge traversing another side ravine. These bridges carry pedestrian traffic and sewer lines across the gaps where these side ravines interrupt the path of NE 61st Street. `WWW`

At the far side of the bridge, climb 28 steps, emerging onto NE 61st Street. You're now walking along the north rim of Ravenna Ravine. As you walk west along NE 61st Street, you'll see 21st Avenue NE coming from the right, toward a steel traffic barrier at the ravine's edge. At the far end of the barrier, take the gravel path angling to the left that parallels 61st Street along the north edge of the ravine and then runs into a pedestrian/bicycle-only bridge at 20th Avenue NE. Turn left (south) onto this bridge to cross the main ravine (5). `WWW`

This magnificent steel bridge was built in 1913 and closed to auto traffic in 1975. It is on the National Register of Historic Places, along with another bridge crossing the ravine farther to the west, at 15th Avenue NE. If you decide to take the optional Upper Ravine Loop, you'll get a wonderful view of both bridges from below.

From the bridge you'll have great views up and down the ravine, including the main path running down the center of the ravine along Ravenna Creek. Note the smaller parallel paths flanking the main path on either side of the ravine. We'll refer to these later.

Continue south just past the end of the bridge, and follow the gravel path curving to the left back to the wide grassy picnic area (3) at the top of the same timber stairway you took down into the ravine.

For the optional side route to Cowen Park at the head of the ravine, study the map chiseled into the sign near the top of the stairs for an overview of the Upper Ravine Loop that runs beneath the two bridges. (WWW) This adds 0.8 mile round-trip (see "Option: Upper Ravine Loop").

Ravenna Ravine North Trail: Head once more down the now-familiar timber stairs and back into the ravine. Cross the small footbridge over Ravenna Creek as before. Take a few steps upstream (west) along the central trail, watching for a side trail marked "RAVENNA PARK TRAIL SYSTEM NE 58TH STREET." Here, you can choose whether to stick to the main route or take the optional Upper Ravine Loop. For the main route, turn right onto the NE 58th Street trail, and take the right fork that soon appears (6). This "north trail" runs along the ravine's northern slope, parallel to the central trail. At this point you'll be heading southeast, downstream.

This portion of the route is pedestrian-only, so it's quieter, in among the trees and shrubs. Here you'll see the mature results of the daylighting and restoration work that's been done up and down the ravine. In springtime look for skunk cabbages with their yellow, spearhead-like blooms in wetter parts of the landscape. Eventually, you'll cross a wooden walkway to rejoin the central trail (7), after which the ravine turns south and opens out at the lower end. (WWW)

Option: Upper Ravine Loop

This 0.8-mile-round-trip side trip takes you to Cowen Park, at the head of the ravine. You'll also get great views of the 20th Avenue NE Bridge, this time towering high above. For orientation, remember that the ravine has one broad, east–west central trail with two smaller parallel trails running along the north and south slopes. Connector trails tie these three parallel trails together at various intervals, so it's easy and fun to get "lost" and "found" again.

Continue along the main trail past the side trail marked "RAVENNA PARK TRAIL SYSTEM NE 58TH STREET." Your side trip begins and ends here, as you continue up the main trail heading west, and upstream. You'll pass the side trail you took earlier (marked "RAVENNA PARK TRAIL SYSTEM NE 62ND STREET") and walk beneath the 20th Avenue footbridge you crossed just a few minutes before (5).

You eventually pass under a second bridge, this one a major street carrying auto traffic. Built by the Works Progress Administration (WPA) in 1936, the 15th Avenue NE Bridge is on the National Register of Historic Places. Just beyond it is the end of the trail where the ravine "surfaces," opening up into Cowen Park.

20th Avenue footbridge across Ravenna Ravine

Begin the return part of your loop along the same central trail you came up. Soon after you pass under the 15th Avenue NE Bridge, you have two options for heading down-ravine. The more adventuresome is to take the connector trail heading up to the right just after the bridge (not shown on map). This will quickly put you onto the less-traveled "south trail" that follows the ravine midway up the south slope, with glimpses of the central trail running in parallel below. The second option (as mapped) is to stay on the central trail close beside Ravenna Creek, where you'll get better views of the extensive daylighting and restoration work done by volunteers over recent years.

If you choose to return along the south trail, you'll eventually reach and cross the familiar footbridge over Ravenna Creek to merge with the main trail. In either case, from the central trail, turn up the side trail marked "RAVENNA PARK TRAIL SYSTEM NE 58th STREET." Then pick up the directions for the return segment along the Ravenna Ravine North Trail (6). ♦

Down the Drain: After rejoining the central trail (7), you'll see more of the extensive daylighting and restoration work along Ravenna Creek, just beyond the log fence on your left. Meanwhile, the ravine itself starts to open up, and soon the creek disappears down a pipeline to Union Bay, in the middle of a lovely restored pond and wetland. **WWW** At the very end of the ravine is a ballfield, with NE 55th Street beyond. Here, your Ravenna stairway walk comes full circle.

2 Fremont

Fremont proclaims itself the "center of the universe" and does what it can to live up to its Latin-like motto: *De libertas quirkas*, or "Freedom to be peculiar." Its mixed image—funky and weird, with a dollop of hipster—makes Fremont a destination for visitors and natives alike. It's a remarkable outcome for a neighborhood that during 120 years of existence has been battered by one socioeconomic upheaval after another, played out in a tiny crucible of just 1.4 square miles.

The Lake Washington Ship Canal marks the southern border of Fremont, and also its lowest elevation. The terrain rises to the north, jumping from one small hill to another in the direction of Phinney Ridge. With these hills go stairways, and this walk traverses many of them, gaining and losing about 300 feet along the way. You'll start with a short stroll along the Burke-Gilman Trail, which runs scenically alongside the Ship Canal here. Turning away from the canal you'll head north, climbing gradually up the residential streets and stairways to Fremont Peak Park, near the northern limits of the neighborhood. After enjoying the park's stunning views you'll head back, exploring a charming series of stairs and narrow lanes along the eastern side of the neighborhood before turning back to the eclectic commercial center, home of the famous Lenin statue and the Fremont rocket.

This stairway walk reveals different facets of Fremont: blue-collar, artsy-bohemian, and high-tech. An optional side trip to tourist destinations like the *Fremont Troll* and the *Waiting for the Interurban* sculptures also takes you past the beautifully refurbished Carnegie-era Fremont Library with its art-filled spiral plaza, down an elegantly curving stairway next to the library, and gives you a close look at the historic Fremont drawbridge.

If you do both the main and the side routes, you'll come away with a wide-angle view of this very complicated, lively, scenic Seattle neighborhood.

Length:	**3.2 miles (add 0.75 mile with optional walk)**
Walking Time:	1 hour 30 minutes (add 45 minutes with optional walk)
Steps Down:	224 (add 86 with optional Attractions of Commercial District walk)
Steps Up:	302
Kid-Friendly:	Kids will enjoy the Ship Canal at the beginning, and Fremont Peak Park in the middle. The entire loop may be a bit tiring.
Cafes/Pubs:	Canal Street Coffee, along the Ship Canal, has a comfortable porch overlooking a small garden, a great place for sitting and watching passersby along the canal.

Getting There: There is free 2-hour street parking in the area where Phinney Avenue N intersects N 34th Street/N Canal Street. On Sundays the nearby Fremont Street Market starts at 10 AM, which can make finding parking a bit more complicated. If you're taking the bus, Metro Transit Routes 26 and 28 (from Downtown Seattle) and MT31 (University District and Magnolia) have nearby stops. You'll start the walk by heading south on Phinney toward the Ship Canal.

The Burke-Gilman Trail and the Ship Canal: As you approach the start of the walk, look for Theo Chocolate on the east side of Phinney, as well as the dinosaur topiary where Phinney Avenue N intersects the Burke-Gilman Trail and the Ship Canal. From Phinney, turn right onto the Burke-Gilman Trail, heading northwest beside the canal, with N Canal Street running parallel on the right. For safety, walkers in both directions are expected to stay on the canal side of the trail.

Continue along the Burke-Gilman Trail between Canal Street and the Ship Canal itself. You'll soon spot Canal Street Coffee on your right, where Canal Street merges with N 35th Street and 1st Avenue NW.

Soon after you pass Canal Street Coffee, watch for where Canal Street veers away from the trail, becoming 2nd Avenue NW. Just before this point, on your left, is a canal overlook with a covered seating area WWW, a nice spot to watch canal traffic (1). Follow 2nd Avenue NW away from the Ship Canal for just a few yards to where it opens onto Leary Way NW. Here, make a soft left onto Leary (a hard left puts you onto 3rd Avenue NW).

To the 1st Avenue Stairs (63 steps up): Continue on Leary to the intersection with NW 39th Street. Here you'll encounter a four-way signaled crosswalk. If you cross 39th first and then cross Leary, you'll end up walking east along the north side of 39th Street, in perfect position for the next left turn. You're now leaving the busy commercial part of Fremont for a tour of its quieter residential areas.

Walking east on NW 39th Street, you'll soon pass 2nd Avenue NW. Turn left at the next block, onto 1st Avenue NW. Continue north one block, across NW Bowdoin Place, and you'll see your first stairway straight ahead—the 1st Avenue stairs (2). WWW

To the NW 42nd Street Stairs (32 steps down): After climbing up the 1st Avenue stairs, continue north on 1st Avenue to N 41st Street. Here, 1st Avenue appears to be ending in a T intersection with 41st, but it's just making a jog. Do a zig left onto 41st and a quick zag right, and you'll be back on 1st Avenue N.

Continue north on 1st Avenue for one more block, turning left at N 42nd Street—the top of your next stairway (3). WWW As soon as the street reappears at the bottom, turn right onto 2nd Avenue NW.

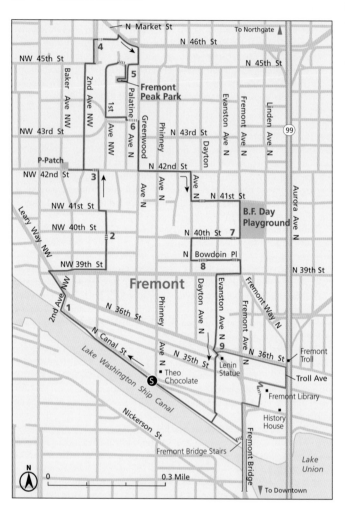

To the NW 46th Street Stairs (86 steps up): Walk three blocks north on 2nd Avenue NW, which ends in a T intersection with NW 45th Street. Turn right onto 45th, then left at the next block, onto 1st Avenue NW. Here, 1st Avenue splits in two, with one lane running along the high side of the hill. Stay on the low-side lane, walking north along the narrow sidewalk. Traffic goes two ways

FREMONT: RISE, FALL, AND RISE AGAIN

Fremont was platted as a new development in 1888, and it was a successful industry-oriented neighborhood from the start. With mills and an iron foundry spurring quick growth, Fremont was absorbed by the City of Seattle just three years after it was founded.

Like many Seattle neighborhoods, Fremont's early fortunes depended on connections with the nearby communities scattered widely about the area. It gained local rail and streetcar service around 1890, and in 1910 the new interurban rail line between Seattle and Everett created a stop here—as commemorated by the *Waiting for the Interurban* statue in the commercial district. In 1917 the new Fremont Bridge started operating and the Ship Canal opened to marine traffic. All these links helped Fremont grow rapidly; most of the older buildings you'll see in the business district date from this prosperous period, spanning the first two decades of the century.

Unfortunately for Fremont, in 1932 the Aurora Bridge opened. This allowed traffic between Seattle and parts north to zip along high overhead, bypassing Fremont entirely. In 1939 the interurban rail line closed as it became clear that cars and trucks were the favored way to move people and goods up and down the Sound. These transportation decisions, made elsewhere, badly damaged Fremont's connections with the rest of the region and started the neighborhood down a long road of decline.

Fremont made a big comeback, though. Today it's an offbeat and artsy place for both locals and tourists to visit. It's also a high-tech jobs center, with companies like Google, Adobe, and Getty Images maintaining offices here.

Two major players seem largely responsible for that transformation. Well into the 1970s, Fremont was a low-rent haven for craftspeople, artists, and students. The Fremont Arts Council (FAC) formed in 1978 to put local artistic energies and talents to work enlivening the neighborhood. Through various grants and commissions, FAC is responsible for many local attractions like the *Waiting for the Interurban* sculpture and the Fremont Troll. It also produces the Solstice Parade, which attracts tens of thousands of visitors to Fremont each June.

The other major mover in Fremont is Suzie Burke, scion of a Fremont mill-owning family. In the 1980s and '90s she bought up depressed properties throughout Fremont, turning many of them into high-tech developments. Today, Adobe occupies the site where her family's mill used to be.

Many old-time residents grumble that development has been the ruin of Fremont, raising rents and destroying the old bohemian ambience. Others embrace the changes as evidence that Fremont has finally mastered the economic winds that battered it for so many decades.

on both the high and low sides, so keep an eye out. In a few yards you'll come to NW 46th Street, with a set of stairs to your right (4). **WWW**

To Fremont Peak Park and N 45th Street Stairs (95 steps down): Climb the first flight of the NW 46th Street stairs, pausing to check traffic before crossing the upper lane of 1st Avenue NW. After climbing the final flight, the street reappears under a slightly different name (N 46th Street), having moved to the east side of 1st Avenue NW.

Angle over to the sidewalk on the right side of 46th, walking uphill. As the sidewalk curves right, 46th veers away from you to the left where it merges with busy N Market Street. Continue up the sidewalk, walking along a retaining wall just below the level of Market/46th. The sidewalk gradually rises to the level of the street, just on the other side of a guardrail. At Greenwood Avenue N turn right, away from Market/46th.

Fremont Peak Park entrance: Phases of the Moon

THE STORY OF FREMONT PEAK PARK

Fremont Peak Park is a real point of pride in Fremont and an inspiring story of neighborhood activism. The property was originally the site of three houses, with an amazing view toward the Olympic Mountains. When the owner put the property on the market, one local resident, Jack Tomkinson, saw its potential as a park and approached the city. The city agreed to develop a park at the site, but only if it could be taken off the market long enough for city gears to start turning. With a lot of moving and shaking from Suzie Burke and the newly formed Friends of Fremont Peak Park, all three parcels were purchased, the property was preserved, and development of the park soon began.

The park opened in November 2007. It's filled with whimsical touches like the phases of the moon depicted in white stone inserts in the black asphalt park entrance, and a metal planting border that escapes the ground and corkscrews wildly on its own. When we met Jack Tomkinson at the park, he pointed out other features like the "Sunrise Terrace" at the southeast corner, where friends can sit for a cup of coffee in the morning sun, and the remnants of the houses' concrete foundations, incorporated into the landscaping. The park is filled with references to the ancient myth of Theseus, Ariadne, and the Minotaur, including an abstract labyrinth and Ariadne's unfurling spool of thread. A complete description of the park's mythological and astronomical references can be found at the website of the lead artist, Laura Haddad, at www.haddad-drugan.com/projects.html.

Walk through the park to a plaza promontory on the west border of the property for another highlight. From here, if weather allows, you'll get spectacular views of the Ship Canal, Fishermen's Terminal, and Magnolia Hill in the foreground, and Puget Sound and the Olympic Mountains beyond. **WWW**

Walk south on Greenwood for just one block, turning right onto N 45th Street, which continues west a short way before ending with a 90-degree turn to the left. The top of a stairway lies straight ahead, just beyond a traffic guardrail and probably one or two parked cars. You'll return to it, but for now follow the street as it turns left and becomes Palatine Avenue N.

A couple of houses later you arrive at Fremont Peak Park on the right (west) side of Palatine (5). After exploring Fremont Peak Park and its views, head back up Palatine to the top of the stairway you noted at N 45th Street, and descend its 95 steps. **WWW**

A REAL-LIFE CHOCOLATE FACTORY

On the east side of Phinney, a few dozen yards north of the Burke-Gilman Trail is the headquarters of Theo Chocolate, the first organic-chocolate maker in the U.S. Here select cocoa beans from around the world are roasted and processed into a variety of chocolate bars and confections. You can take an all-ages tour of the plant, where in a little over an hour you'll learn all about the process from "bean to bar" and get the opportunity to sample most of their products. Reservations are required for weekend tours. The Theo Chocolate building previously housed the Redhook Brewery and before that, until 1941, was the Fremont Trolley Barn.

To the N 43rd Street Stairs (59 steps up): At the bottom of the N 45th Street stairs, continue straight ahead for 20 yards. Stay with the street as it curves downhill to the left, turning into 1st Avenue NW. Turn left at the next intersection (where streets merge from several directions), onto N 43rd Street.

At this point N 43rd Street's two lanes of opposing traffic are separated by a wide, brush- and tree-covered median. After one block N 43rd Street ends, at Palatine Avenue N. Your next set of stairs lies straight ahead (6). **WWW**

To the N 40th Street Stairs (72 steps up, 66 steps down): At the top of the N 43rd Street stairs, turn right onto Greenwood Avenue N. Continue south on Greenwood for one and a half blocks, turning left onto N 42nd Street. Walk east on N 42nd Street for three blocks, then turn right on Dayton Avenue N.

Head downhill and south for one block on Dayton Avenue, turning left onto N 41st Street, which at this point is a concrete walkway. You'll traverse a short flight of 20 stairs before the street reappears. Continue straight ahead on N 41st Street for one and a half blocks, turning right onto busy Fremont Avenue N.

Walk south one block on Fremont, then turn right at the base of the stairs at N 40th Street (7). The stairway is marked by a signaled crosswalk, with the campus of B. F. Day School across the street. Opened in 1892, it's Seattle's longest-operating elementary school.

Note the tilework at the base of these stairs. The sculpted steel balustrades are reminiscent of the Fremont Bridge's steel girders, which you'll view soon, if you take the side trip. **WWW** Halfway up is a landing, where two small apartment buildings form a cozy, decorative courtyard.

Once you've reached the top of this first stairway, continue ahead on N 40th Street, crossing Evanston Avenue N. After you cross Evanston, slightly hidden but just ahead is the second of the N 40th Street stairs. Take these curving steps down.

To the N Bowdoin Place Stairs and Back to the Canal (40 steps up, 31 steps down): Once at the bottom of the second N 40th Street stairway, continue ahead on N 40th Street for one block, turning left onto Dayton Avenue N. At the next block, turn left again, onto N Bowdoin Place, where you'll see another set of stairs straight ahead (8). Up you go! **WWW**

At the top of this first set of Bowdoin stairs you'll emerge onto a narrow lane, with a small apartment building on the right. Continue straight ahead, once again passing Evanston Avenue N, which now comes in from your left but stops here, in deference to the steep hill dropping off to your right.

Continue along the lane, and soon you'll see an alley on the left followed by a charming cedar-shake shingled house, right next to the top of the second set of Bowdoin stairs. The steps are interspersed with sections of steep concrete walkway, to which someone has very helpfully fixed rubber treads for traction. At the bottom of the stairs turn right, heading south once again on Fremont Avenue.

One-half block along Fremont, you'll arrive at a traffic light and a three-way intersection where Fremont Avenue N, N 39th Street, and Fremont Way N come together. Take the signaled crosswalk across N 39th Street, then turn right on the other side, walking west on 39th.

Walk to the next block, passing a steep dirt alleyway on your left before turning left onto Evanston Avenue N. Head south along the east side of Evanston, all the way to the next major intersection at N 36th Street. Take the signaled crosswalk toward the 16-foot tall statue of a heroically forward-striding V. I. Lenin (9). **WWW**

THE FAMOUS FREMONT LENIN STATUE

The Lenin statue (9), a rescued relic of the end of the Soviet era, seems to embody Fremont's motto, *De libertas quirkas*. After all, what other neighborhood would feel so free to welcome this quirky landmark? The statue was commissioned to a Bulgarian sculptor for a prominent spot in a square in Poprad, Czechoslovakia, but in a case of horrible timing, it was installed in 1988—one year before the fall of the country's Communist regime.

The statue was quietly removed from its place and sent to a scrapyard, where it was discovered by Lewis Carpenter, an Issaquah resident who happened to be teaching English in the town. He bought the statue and shipped it to Seattle, mortgaging his house to do it. Mr. Carpenter died shortly thereafter, and the statue was left lying in his backyard until the family found this spot in Fremont.

Today the Lenin statue is a well-known Fremont landmark, though it remains up for sale. It's often decorated with a red star during the holidays and dressed up in drag during Pride Week. For the 2004 Solstice Parade it silently reviewed the marchers—dressed up as John Lennon.

When you finish contemplating Lenin, take a moment to view the patio just behind him—specifically, the caulking between the tiles, which is embedded with all kinds of miscellaneous items, like old watches, dinnerware, jewelry, etc. Then, you can either take a side trip to see more of the quirky tourist attractions for which Fremont is so well known, or you can make your way back to your starting place. To take the optional walk, see "Option: Attractions of the Commercial District."

To return directly to your starting place, step onto the adjoining crosswalk and head south across Fremont Place. Continue south on Evanston for one block, where at the southeast corner of N 35th Street you'll see the famous Fremont Rocket. It's said to be made of a surplus Fairchild C-119 tail boom, gussied up with fins and other rocket-like accoutrements.

Evanston comes to an end at a T intersection with N Northlake Way. Cross Northlake, and walk onto the plaza straight ahead. Google's Seattle offices face the plaza from the left. Continue down the plaza steps to the Burke-Gilman Trail, turning right onto the trail. From there, head west to your starting point.

Option: Attractions of the Commercial District (86 steps down)

An additional 0.75-mile walk includes the better-known tourist attractions in Fremont. **WWW** The side trip starts from the Lenin statue (9) and takes you back to your starting place along a slightly different route.

From the Lenin statue, walk east along N 36th Street for four blocks. When it's safe and convenient, move over to the north side of the street. Soon you'll see the Aurora Bridge looming ahead. Continue under the bridge, where you'll see the resident Troll lurking under the abutment, munching on its latest meal. **WWW** Be careful not to stand in the right-of-way at the traffic diversion there!

Walk south on Troll Avenue, which runs along the bridge. Turn right at the next block, onto N 35th Street. Halfway down the block on your left you'll see the white, Mission Revival Fremont Library. The library is on the National Register of Historic Places and has been named a landmark by Seattle's Landmarks Preservation Board. It was built in 1921 on a Carnegie grant and, along with many libraries in Seattle, was renovated in 2005 under the "Libraries for All" bond measure. **WWW**

Just west of the library, turn into A. B. Ernst Park. Ambrose Ernst is considered the father of the city's playfields. As a parks commissioner, he played a key role in implementing the Olmsted Parks Plan after 1906. The park is a spiral-shaped plaza with beautiful xeriscaping, seating areas, and an interesting sculpture called *Water Mover* (if it's raining, you'll see why). At the far end of the park head down the curving 38-step stairway. At the bottom continue straight ahead, through a parking lot, to N 34th Street.

Waiting for the Interurban *in Fremont*

Here, you can take a brief detour to the left, where History House is located on the next corner. It contains all sorts of historical materials about Fremont and other Seattle neighborhoods, and runs a variety of special events, such as a summer music series.

To continue, turn right onto 34th, heading west for a halfblock. Just before you reach Fremont Avenue N, look south across the street to see the *Waiting for the Interurban* sculpture by Richard Beyer, a cast-aluminum sculpture of six waiting passengers, installed in 1979 in commemoration of the old Seattle-to-Everett interurban rail line. The figures are often draped in or supplemented by additional pieces of art or whimsy. (Fremont residents call these and other temporary installations "art attacks;" History House has an exhibit of some of the best *Waiting for the Interurban* enhancements over the years.)

After passing the statue, cross Fremont Avenue N at the signaled crosswalk. Then take its perpendicular partner at the opposite side, crossing over to the southwest corner of Fremont and 34th. This is a good place to turn around and look west along 34th for the extraordinary Gaudi look-alike building that houses PCC Natural Market and a condo development. **WWW**

Head south on Fremont Avenue toward the Fremont Bridge. You'll pass Getty Images' global headquarters on the right, and soon the canal comes into view. Just before the bridge, on the right you'll see the top of a set of metal stairs. **WWW** Take these stairs down to the canal and the Burke-Gilman Trail. Return to your starting place by walking away from the bridge, heading west. ◆

HISTORIC FREMONT BRIDGE

Fremont Bridge opened in June 1917, just a month before the Ship Canal opened to marine traffic between Lake Washington and Puget Sound. Before then, a wood trestle bridge connected Fremont with lower Queen Anne Hill. This beloved landmark, with its unique, citizen-voted blue and orange colors, is listed on the National Register of Historic Places. **WWW** It's also a major irritant to local drivers: because marine traffic has the right-of-way under federal rules, the bridge is raised about 35 times a day. This makes the Fremont Bridge one of the busiest bascule ("seesaw") bridges in the world. There are three other bascules along the canal: the Ballard, University, and Montlake bridges, all built within eight years of one another.

3 Golden Gardens

If you're looking for a short stairway walk, this is a great choice. Though it can be covered in less than an hour, the scenery and ambience vary widely along multiple stairways and paths, from the Loyal Heights neighborhood to Golden Gardens beach, 300 feet below.

As you zigzag down the bluff, there's an excellent chance you'll spot a bald eagle soaring overhead, or hear the barks of California sea lions drifting up from their marina hangout far below. At one point the rate of descent slows and a brook suddenly appears alongside your stairway route. When you reach the bottom, you'll duck into a colorfully decorated tunnel leading beneath the busy Burlington Northern train tracks and onto the Golden Gardens beach. Here the route skirts grass-covered dunes before threading between two small and waterbird-rich freshwater ponds, just yards away from the salty Sound.

While the walk itself is short, it's easy to find excuses to linger at the beach. The mountains and sound are magnificent, the birding and train-spotting are great, and the people-watching is especially entertaining in the warmer months, when this beach is one of the city's prime destinations. It's also fun to stake out a random sunset, and discreetly toast whatever the result may be.

The walk starts in a central location convenient to other attractions in the nearby North Beach/Blue Ridge, Crown Hill, and Sunset Hill neighborhoods. It's easy to extend your visit to explore a hidden stairway park tucked into a street-end, view a totem pole in a butterfly garden, or check out favored local viewpoints of the mountains and Sound. You'll find directions to these additional highlights at our book website. **WWW**

Path to Golden Gardens' shoreline

Length:	**1.4 miles**
Walking Time:	Less than 1 hour
Steps Down:	272
Steps Up:	272 (it's an out-and-back route)
Kid-Friendly:	This beach destination is great for older kids who can handle the 300-foot elevation gain and loss (and there are trains, too!).
Cafes/Pubs:	Caffè Fiore is a neighborhood hangout right at the starting point, with good coffee and pastries; there's also a seasonal snack bar at the beach. Other places are within driving distance.

Getting There: You can find free parking on NW 85th Street, just east of 32nd Avenue NW and close to the top of the first stairway. MT 48 stops near 32nd and 85th, arriving via Capitol Hill, Mount Baker, the University District, Green Lake, and Greenwood.

Upper Bluff Stairs (134 steps down): From the south side of NW 85th Street, walk west along the vintage 1908 building that houses Caffè Fiore, then take the crosswalk across 32nd Avenue NW, heading straight onto the gravel path where your walk begins.

The top of the first flight of stairs (1) appears almost immediately **WWW**, leading down into the trees. At the bottom, follow the path left, traversing south down the side of the bluff. The path switchbacks north as shown on the map, still angling downslope toward the second flight of Upper Bluff stairs. This flight

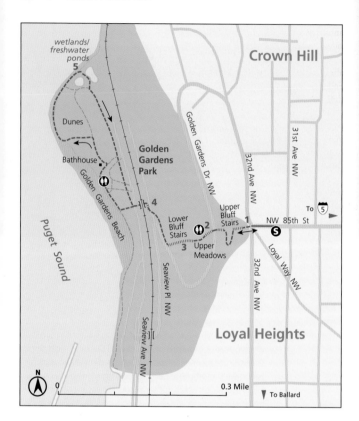

ends at Golden Gardens Drive, which will cross your path again as it winds its own way down the bluff.

Upper Meadows of Golden Gardens Park (16 steps down): Right at the bottom of the Upper Bluff stairs, cross Golden Gardens Drive, using the marked crosswalk. Drivers can't see you until you step off the last stair, so use caution. Once across the street, step down 16 stairs and into the upper meadows area of Golden Gardens Park (2). Follow the path between an enclosed off-leash dog park on your right and a parking lot on your left. Just past restrooms on your right, you'll find your next stairway, the Lower Bluff stairs (3). **WWW**

Lower Bluff Stairs (108 steps down): These stairs run charmingly beside a channelized brook. Unfortunately, the waters of this stream aren't pristine (perhaps due to the off-leash area above), so keep kids away. At the bottom of these stairs Golden Gardens Drive passes by again as it completes another switchback. This time you don't cross, but instead turn right onto the sidewalk next to the street.

Golden Gardens Drive hairpins sharply away to your left while, straight ahead, an overflow parking area for the Golden Gardens beach comes into view. Follow the painted walkway into the parking area as it angles to the left side of the lot.

Tunnel Stairs to the Beach (14 steps down): At the left edge of the overflow lot, look for a cobblestoned incline leading down to a short stairway. You'll see a twin stairway coming down from the opposite side. At the bottom of these opposing stairs is a lavishly decorated tunnel entrance (4). Continue through the tunnel under the railroad tracks, and out the other side. `WWW`

As you come out of the tunnel, take the sidewalk straight ahead past some trees on the right side, until you arrive at a small concrete plaza decorated with colorful inlaid "swoops." From here you can survey the beach ahead as well as the Sound and Olympic Mountains beyond. Take the sidewalk to the right, toward historic Golden Gardens Bathhouse.

The bathhouse was built in 1929 as a changing area for swimmers at the newly opened municipal park. In 2004 it was renovated using Pro Parks Levy funds. Today it's a community and event center, and listed as a Seattle Landmark. `WWW`

Walk past the bathhouse, following a sidewalk that hugs the landward side of the building. In a few yards you'll notice a broad, log-lined path heading out to the beach. `WWW` Take this path toward the water, walking beside grass-covered dunes.

CAPSULE HISTORY OF LOYAL HEIGHTS

The story of the Loyal Heights neighborhood centers around its founder, Harry Treat, and one of his daughters, Loyal, who lent her name to the neighborhood. Treat had already built a sizable fortune in real estate on the East Coast and in Europe before he moved to Seattle in 1905. Sensing further opportunity in a growing port city, he built a thirty-room mansion (today a fifteen-unit luxury apartment building) in lower Queen Anne, and began casting around for real estate development opportunities.

Treat bought 180 acres of old-growth forestlands perched above the beach north of Ballard. Like so many other "build it and they will come" developers in Seattle, he built an electric trolley line there, along today's Loyal Way NW. At the end of the line, where this stairway walk begins, Treat would put his visitors on a horse-drawn carriage and take them on a winding road down the bluff to "Loyal Beach," the family's private park. In 1922 the city bought Loyal Beach from Treat's estate, and in 1927 recommissioned it as Golden Gardens Park.

Dunes and Ponds: When you reach the beach, turn right, making your way northwest between water and dunes. Soon the beach curves to the right. Just before it runs up against the base of the bluff and the train tracks, you'll see two wooden walkways coming up on the right (5). Take the second of these walkways, heading into a vegetated wetland area between two small freshwater ponds. This area has been the object of intensive clearing and native revegetation efforts in recent years. WWW

Golden Gardens, both on the shoreline and the bluff, supports migrant and resident populations of birds and waterfowl, such as eagles, ospreys, woodpeckers, and American widgeons, not to mention many terrestrial creatures. Although human activity has chipped away at their habitat for over a hundred years, these ponds and the forested areas above are now being painstakingly restored through continuing efforts of groups like the Washington Native Plant Society and EarthCorps. Volunteering opportunities are listed on Golden Gardens page at Seattle Parks' website, www.seattle.gov/parks.

Heading south from the ponds, the path leads you past an open grassy area on your right and toward the tunnel. Retrace your steps through the tunnel and up the bluff to your starting point. WWW Once you've topped the Upper Bluff stairs, your walk is at an end, though you might want to explore the additional attractions in nearby neighborhoods. WWW

4　Cedar Park and the Burke-Gilman Trail

Cedar Park is a quiet neighborhood that spills over the bluff at the north end of Lake Washington. Part of the fun of this walk comes from exploring a scenic but decidedly out-of-the-way neighborhood: it's right at the northern edge of the city limits; streets are scarce down the bluff; and the eastern side of the neighborhood ends at lake's edge.

The walk initially descends a long, steep stairway with great views of the lake. A quiet, hidden path links two more stairways that bring you down to the Burke-Gilman Trail, which you'll follow north along the lake for a mile or so. Then, as you climb back up the bluff, you can check out how the local residents adapt their homes and yards for maximum enjoyment of the sloping topography and views.

In most of Seattle around the turn of the last century, stairways were built to connect new hillside developments to trolley lines. In contrast Cedar Park, along with the adjoining neighborhoods in the Lake City district, is young enough to have been built around automobile transport. This is probably why there are so few stairways here, though this walk covers the major ones. If time is a limiting

NE 130th Street stairs down to the Burke-Gilman Trail (Dave Ralph)

factor, consider the shortcut option that keeps all the stairs but truncates the neighborhood meander up from the Burke-Gilman Trail.

Length:	**3.2 miles (1.7 miles with A Shorter Option)**
Walking Time:	About 1 hour 30 minutes (50 minutes with A Shorter Option)
Steps Down:	275
Steps Up:	196
Kid-Friendly:	Cedar Park has play equipment and a portable toilet; nearby stairs have landings and walkways; kids may prefer the shortcut option.
Cafes/Pubs:	Bring your own on this walk! There are picnic tables at Cedar Park.

Getting There: There's a parking lot at the Cedar Park starting point (3737 NE 135th Street). Several Metro Transit Routes stop at Lake City Way NE and NE 137th Street, about a third of a mile from the starting point. These bus routes run from Downtown (MT306, MT312, ST522); Lake City (MT330); the U District (MT372); Shoreline City College (MT330) and Woodinville (ST522).

To the NE 135th Stairs (196 steps down): From Cedar Park, head east on NE 135th Street, walking slightly uphill. Just past 40th Avenue NE watch for a guardrail straight ahead, marking the street-end. To the right of the guardrail

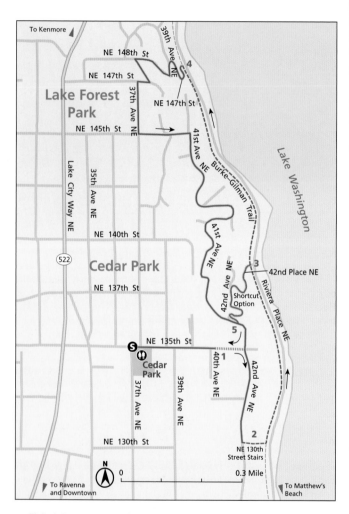

you'll find the entrance to the NE 135th stairs (1). These lengthy stairs are the beginning of your trek down the bluff toward Lake Washington.

After the first flight the rate of descent eases, and a concrete walkway briefly intervenes. On the right look for an interesting retaining wall, built from chunks of concrete the city repurposed from somewhere else. Over the years it has slowly turned into an extravagantly textured hanging-moss garden. WWW

Watch for nice glimpses of the northern reaches of Lake Washington to the left, over the treetops.

To the Hidden NE 130th Stairs (79 steps down): On reaching the bottom of the NE 135th stairs, turn right onto 42nd Avenue NE. After curving gently to the right, 42nd runs gently downhill. Past a second curve, watch for a speed-bump sign. On the left is a guardrail and then, just past the speed bump, an opening in the traffic barrier. This is your gateway to the NE 130th Street stairs (2), leading to the Burke-Gilman Trail and Lake Washington. `WWW`

At the bottom of the first flight, the stairs turn into a paved walkway through an open, ravine-like passage between houses. Midway along the path, a charming little brook comes in from the left, dives into a channel underground, and crosses under your feet just as you start down the final flight of stairs to the Burke-Gilman Trail. `WWW`

The Burke-Gilman Trail: At the bottom of the NE 130th Street stairs, turn left. You'll stroll north alongside Lake Washington for about a mile, threading between the steep, forested bluff and custom lakeside homes. Runners and bicyclists regularly use the trail, so keep an eye out, and stay to the right. If you're in a group, take care not to spread across the trail.

Watch for 42nd Place NE, on the left (3). This marks your midway point along the Burke-Gilman Trail before you head uphill to explore the neighborhood above. However, you can trim 1.5 miles by turning off the trail right here and heading back on 42nd Place NE, following the directions under "A Shorter Option."

To continue with the complete route, keep walking past 42nd Place. Then, after strolling the Burke-Gilman Trail for another 0.5 mile, take a left at the signed NE 147th Street (4).

Back to the Bluff: As it climbs the bluff away from the trail, NE 147th makes sharp switchbacks and undergoes a dizzying series of name changes. There are also lots of opportunities to check out the eclectic and ingenious landscaping in the neighborhood.

When you get to the second house on your right, turn left onto 39th Avenue NE (at a ⊤ intersection). After you turn onto 39th, the street curves very sharply to the right, and briefly runs along as 38th Place NE before changing names again, this time to NE 148th Street. Continue up for another block as the street curves more gently to the left, then turn left onto 38th Avenue NE.

From here, stay on the main road as it curves right and becomes NE 147th Street. Almost immediately, turn left onto 37th Avenue NE. Walk south on 37th for one block, then turn left onto NE 145th Street.

At this point you'll be briefly heading east on 145th, with Lake Washington in view straight ahead. Walk past the signed 38th Avenue NE on your right, continuing until the street curves to the right, signed at this point as 40th Avenue NE.

THE BURKE-GILMAN TRAIL

The old railroad route that is today's Burke-Gilman Trail was conceived in 1885 as the Seattle, Lake Shore, and Eastern Railway (SLS & E). Thomas Burke, Daniel Gilman, and other investors had a great ambition: to build a Seattle-based railroad with transcontinental connections. At first, local lines carried coal and timber, but by 1892 the group succeeded in making a border connection with Canadian Pacific's transcontinental railroad.

Over time, the old SLS & E went through a series of owners, culminating with Burlington Northern Railroad (BN), which in 1970 announced it would abandon the line. A visionary citizen's group successfully urged the city to convert the right-of-way to a public pedestrian and bicycle trail, and by 1978 it extended 12 miles between Gas Works Park and Bothell. Sections have been added from Gas Works Park through Fremont, skipping the industrial heart of Ballard (due to ongoing litigation), then continuing from Hiram M. Chittenden Locks all the way up to Golden Gardens (see walk 3, "Golden Gardens"). Filling in the 1.5 miles of "Ballard gap" would provide uninterrupted, mostly paved trail from Golden Gardens Park all the way to Issaquah, more than 42 miles!

This section of the trail is interesting year-round. **WWW** In the cooler seasons, when the trees are bare and sight lines are unobstructed, you can spot signs of chronic land slippage along the bluff—trees leaning downhill or patches of bare, disturbed earth. A lot of water percolates through the bluffs down to the lake, so this is prime landslide territory. In summer, walkers, skaters, bicyclists, and occasionally three-wheeled "carving" scooters share the trail. Matthews Beach, 2 miles south (at 22 acres, Seattle's largest freshwater beach), is a popular destination along the trail. The Burke-Gilman Trail carries more than 2000 people each day, 75 percent of them on bicycles. It connects neighborhoods and makes car-free trips practical for nearby residents.

There's plenty of wildlife in the woods and wetlands lining the trail, though you'll need patience to see it. Depending on the season pileated woodpeckers, Cooper's hawks, barn owls, bats, and band-tailed pigeons can be seen. Earthbound creatures like burrowing mountain beavers, long-toed salamanders, and Pacific tree frogs live around here too.

NE 135th Street stairs heading back up to Cedar Park

As you walk downhill along 40th Avenue NE, the road switches names, becoming 41st Avenue NE. You'll continue along 41st Avenue NE for about 0.75 mile, winding back and forth and going up and down a bit while generally following the contour of the bluff. Though fairly narrow, this is a main roadway for bluff-side residents, and there are no sidewalks. Watch for traffic!

Back to Cedar Park (196 steps up): Eventually, you'll see another road coming in from the left (5), to join your own route along 41st Avenue NE. The combined roads become 42nd Avenue NE (this is where the shorter route rejoins the main walk). After turning sharply right, the road straightens, and you'll see the familiar 135th Street stairs coming down the hill from your right—the same stairs you descended at the start of your excursion. A few steps ahead on the left is NE 135th Street, heading downhill. Turn right, up the 135th Street stairs, to your starting place at Cedar Park.

A Shorter Option

To enjoy all the stairways with less walking, this alternate route omits some neighborhood sights while reducing your total walking distance by 1.5 miles.

Follow the main route along the Burke-Gilman Trail for 0.5 mile. Then, at the junction with 42nd Place NE (3), turn left and follow the road as it winds up the bluff. About 0.1 mile along, you'll encounter 42nd Avenue NE, which merges from your right. Continue up on 42nd Avenue NE, and in 0.1 mile you'll see 41st Avenue NE coming in from the right. Turn left where the roads merge, now 42nd Avenue NE (5). The road turns sharply to the right,

then straightens, at which point you'll see the 135th Street stairs coming down the hill from your right. These are the stairs you descended at the start of your excursion (a few steps ahead on the left is the signed NE 135th Street, heading downhill). Head up the 135th Street stairs (1) and back to your parking place at Cedar Park. ♦

5 Maple Leaf and Thornton Creek

At 15 miles long, Thornton Creek drains almost 12 square miles of North Seattle, making it the largest watershed and year-round stream in Seattle, second only to Kelsey Creek on the Eastside (see walk 24, "Kelsey Creek Farm and Wilburton Hill"). It wanders through more than 700 backyards and 15 parks and natural areas to Lake Washington, open and aboveground 90 percent of the way. Still, Thornton Creek is way off most Seattleites' radar. That includes local residents, almost 70 percent of whom can't name it.

The creek's low profile isn't helped much by names like "Thornton Creek Water Quality Channel," which hardly hints at the cool mix of approachable public art, striking urban architecture, and sunken gardens you'll see there. Then there's the aptly named "Beaver Pond Natural Area," 7 acres thriving with crawfish, beavers (complete with lodge and dam), great blue herons, wood ducks, and other wildlife.

This walk meanders up the South Fork of Thornton Creek. Away from the route to the east, the South Fork mostly runs over concrete until it reaches Nathan Hale High School, a little over 0.25 mile away. Another 0.25 mile east of the high school, the South Fork meets the North Fork near Meadowbrook Pond, a wildlife refuge and possible side trip. The combined main stem of Thornton Creek then runs another 1.3 mostly channelized miles before it finally empties into Lake Washington at Matthews Beach Park.

The stairways are strong on variety and charm, but sparse in number—only 462 steps, most of them heading down. On the other hand, this is one of the longer walks, with much to discover along the way. The route explores the Maple Leaf and Victory Heights neighborhoods. It takes you to within a stone's throw of Northgate Mall, almost in view of the creek's headwaters, before turning back. You'll stand on the shady banks of Thornton Creek, then peer down on it from a bridge high above. You'll visit a beaver pond teeming with wildlife, then find yourself walking down what seems like a country lane right in the middle of the city. This walk is so kaleidoscopic, it might require multiple viewings to process it all!

Length:	**4.7 miles**
Walking Time:	1 hour 45 minutes
Steps Down:	326
Steps Up:	136
Kid-Friendly:	At almost 5 miles, the full walk is too long for younger kids. However, a great kids' adventure could take in Thornton Creek Water Quality Channel (TCWQC), the Maple Leaf Community Garden, and the Beaver Pond. In addition to the pond, you'll encounter stairs, places to run and climb, colorful public art, and a small labyrinth. Parking is available nearby, as are eateries and restrooms just a few steps north of TCWQC along Thornton Place.
Cafes/Pubs:	There's cafe access midway through the walk, next to the captivating TCWQC.

Getting There: If driving, park on NE 98th Street just east of Ravenna Avenue NE, near the junction of Lake City Way NE and NE 98th Street. If you're riding the bus, Metro Transit Route 72 from Downtown stops at Lake City Way NE and NE 98th Street, right where this walk begins.

Note: Beaver Pond Natural Area and other areas near the creek can be muddy, especially in winter. Plan your footwear with that in mind. Be alert to some traffic too, as you'll be walking along streets without sidewalks and crossing a couple of arterials.

To La Villa Meadows Natural Area: This protected section of the South Fork of Thornton Creek, 4 acres of city-owned greenspace, is just a block or so away from your starting point, tucked discreetly between houses and an unassuming but historically significant storefront. Here, local volunteers are working with the Thornton Creek Alliance to restore native plants along the creek, which will in turn provide shelter and shade for native creek-dwellers. This segment of the route is a side-spur from the main route. It gives you an early glimpse of the

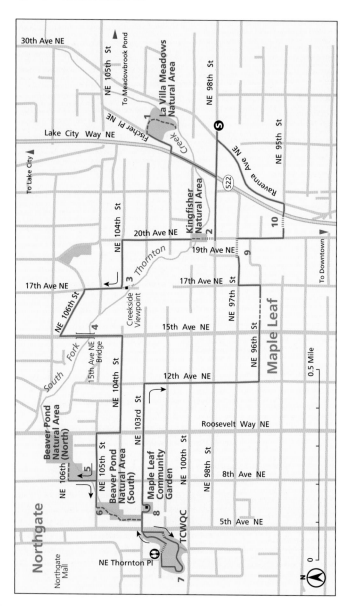

lower reaches of Thornton Creek, a major theme for this walk. However the trail can be a bit overgrown. Some walkers might prefer to skip this part and start with the next segment.

To reach La Villa Meadows Natural Area (1), walk to the junction of NE 98th Street and Lake City Way NE. From the east side of Lake City Way, turn north and walk along the sidewalk, then angle right at Fischer Place NE. Walk a short distance past a small red concrete-block building with "LA VILLA DAIRY" painted along the top. Opened around 1922, this was one of the very first businesses along newly paved Lake City Way, when it was known as "Victory Highway." From the north side of the old dairy, walk to the back, away from the street, to find the path into the trees and to the creek. **WWW** The trail sign may still have the old name: Thornton Creek Natural Area.

To return to the main walk, retrace your steps on Lake City Way, following the sidewalk on the east side. At the stoplighted junction with NE 98th Street, cross to the south side.

To the 20th Avenue NE Stairs and Kingfisher Natural Area (64 steps down): From the south side of NE 98th Street, use the lighted walk to cross busy Lake City Way. This puts you on a sidewalk as you continue west on 98th. Just as you leave the busy junction, peek into the unusual yard of the first house on your left. Here you'll see a circular stone labyrinth, where a sign welcomes you to try it out if you're fourteen or older. **WWW** This house is actually a specialty bookstore.

Past a few more houses, the forest on the right thickens, marking the ravine where the South Fork runs. As you start angling uphill, watch for a guardrail on your right. Soon after, you'll see the top of the 20th Avenue NE stairs (2). These stairs lead down into the ravine and your first crossing of the creek, at Kingfisher Natural Area.

This part of the route is an important crossing for kids getting to and from Sacajawea Elementary School, just a couple of blocks behind you on 20th. At the bottom of the stairs there's a path and a bridge across the creek, which runs through a flat wetland along the ravine bottom. Once over the creek and through the wetland, the path climbs steeply up the other side of the ravine, to the residential area above.

To Creekside Viewpoint, 17th Avenue NE: Continue on 20th Avenue NE to NE 104th Street, and turn left. Walk one block west until 104th ends, just before it would plunge into Thornton Creek. You'll pick up 104th in a few minutes, just on the other side of the creek. Here, though, the street turns 90 degrees to the right, becoming 17th Avenue NE.

Before you head up 17th, this is a good opportunity to see the creek. Directly opposite 17th is a lane heading downhill; it leads to nice views of a broad, open section of the creek (3). Large boulders mark a pathway across—a reason to return for more exploring!

To 15th Avenue NE Bridge Viewpoint: After taking in the creekside view (3), continue north on 17th Avenue NE for two blocks. Then angle left, onto NE 106th Street, walking another block until you reach 15th Avenue NE. Turn left onto 15th and walk south, following the path/sidewalk on the left. Soon you'll reach a bridge (4), with terrific views of the ravine and Thornton Creek far below. Not long ago the bridge was closed and under constant monitoring for foundation cracks as the slope eroded beneath it. After extensive renovation, the bridge reopened in April 2011.

To Beaver Pond Natural Area (North): Just a few steps beyond the bridge (4), look to the right for NE 104th Street. Carefully cross 15th Avenue NE to continue walking west on 104th. After a couple of blocks you'll reach another busy two-lane arterial, Roosevelt Way NE. First cross over, then turn right to walk up the west side of Roosevelt.

After walking just one block north along Roosevelt, turn left onto NE 105th Street, heading west. Continue past 9th Avenue NE on your right; although it does enter Beaver Pond Natural Area, our next stop, it doesn't actually allow access to the beaver pond. After 9th and a few houses, you'll see the thick greenspace on your right that is the Natural Area (5).

Turn right onto 8th Avenue NE and walk north for a block, with the Natural Area on your right and an apartment building on your left. At NE 106th turn right, and here you'll find a number of access points to shoreside views of the beaver pond.

On a weekend, you may find volunteers working in the park, pulling weeds, or planting. Avoiding any recent plantings, you can walk to within a few feet of the pond to catch a view of the beaver lodge **WWW**, a huge pile of sticks and branches. The resident beavers built a dam to back up Thornton Creek and create this pond. To see the dam, go to the end of 106th and bushwhack a few steps in. You may also see a man-made spillover device installed in the dam to prevent neighborhood flooding during heavy rain. This "beaver deceiver" looks like a wire cage sticking out of the pond, with flexible plastic pipe running through to the other side of the dam, allowing water to pass through when levels get high.

Beaver Pond Natural Area (South), Creekside (11 steps up): After you've explored the north part of Beaver Pond Natural Area (5), retrace your steps to the intersection of NE 105th Street and 8th Avenue NE, turning right onto 105th. Here the street narrows to a single lane with an elevated sidewalk along the right side as it crosses over Thornton Creek. It feels like a country lane in the middle of the city!

Watch for an asphalt walkway that branches off the road to the right. Here, look left for the trail into the southern section of Beaver Pond Natural Area (6). In summer when undergrowth is exuberant, the trail may be hard to see until you're almost next to it. In the rainy months, this south section of the Natural Area can get muddy, though improvements to the trail are in the works. Just make sure you have appropriate footwear.

GREAT PLACE FOR WILDLIFE

Much of today's Beaver Pond Natural Area was purchased, parcel by parcel, from private landowners in the late 1970s. To buy the land, the city used money raised by "Forward Thrust," a package of bond initiatives passed by Seattle voters in 1968 and 1970. The area was almost entirely covered by blackberries until Seattle Parks, Seattle Public Utilities, and citizen groups like the Thornton Creek Alliance (www.scn.org/tca) began restoration work in 1992. Volunteers cleared invasive plants from the banks, replanted native groundcover, and put in a variety of native trees and shrubs. They left behind woody debris and "snags," the upright remains of dead trees, to provide shelter for fish, waterfowl, and birds like woodpeckers and wood ducks.

Invasives never sleep, so the work continues, but a cascade of beneficial effects is evident. A key event happened around 2008, when beavers felled trees and built a dam. The raised water level and felled trees established new habitat for other plants and animals, which is why beavers are called a "keystone species." They have made the area hospitable to mallards, hooded mergansers, great blue herons, and fish, including numerous cutthroat trout. Beaver Pond Natural Area has even gained the distinction of sheltering the largest crayfish in the watershed.

The beaver dam has had another unexpected impact: by slowing the flow of Thornton Creek, it has created a natural filtration plant for treating urban impurities washing into the creek from nearby parking lots, roads, and fertilized yards. The Natural Area has become a factor in making a healthier and more fish-friendly watershed, complementing the human-engineered Thornton Creek Water Quality Channel.

Consider delaying your plunge onto the trail to briefly explore the walkway on the opposite side, which ends at 5th Avenue NE next to the Northgate Community Center. There are colorful little sculptures and whimsical birdhouses along the way—definitely part of the "kaleidoscopic" neighborhood experience along Thornton Creek.

Once you're back on the trail, follow it through the thickly wooded south portion of Beaver Pond Natural Area. You'll get glimpses of the Pacific Medical Center on the right. The trail cuts right, around the corner of the building, with a side branch heading to the right and up to the building's parking lot. Keep to the main trail at this point, taking a small bridge across Thornton Creek. Right after you cross the bridge, the trail branches. Take the branch to the right, as the one straight ahead ends quickly at NE 104th Street.

After the turn, the main trail crosses a small tributary to Thornton Creek via stepping stones, where you might see skunk cabbage. **WWW** Soon it curves left, skirting an apartment building on the slope above. After that, you'll find yourself climbing 11 timber stairs to emerge onto NE 103rd Street.

Thornton Creek Water Quality Channel (100 steps up and down): Your next destination is a fascinating blend of art, architecture, and urban nature that most Seattleites have never seen. But first, take a quick glance left from the top of the stairs at NE 103rd Street. A half block up the street is the Maple Leaf Community Garden, marked by a funky round structure with a conical roof. You'll check it out later, but for now, head to the right, along the sidewalk.

Cross 5th Avenue NE at the four-way lighted signal, toward the prominent *Wiggle Posts* sculpture at the corner **WWW**, part of a sidewalk sculptural suite by Benson Shaw. Once there, you'll be standing at the downstream terminus of the Thornton Creek Water Quality Channel (TCWQC).

Next, head south up the sidewalk alongside 5th Avenue NE, toward the Aljoya senior apartment complex. Just as you reach the apartments, take the 36

"Bad Buoys" at the Thornton Creek Water Quality Channel

stairs leading down into the channel. At various points around the channel are information kiosks explaining how TCWQC works; one of them is at the top of these stairs. At the bottom, you'll join a sidewalk that loops around the entire channel (7).

This is a good place for a break. From the western side of the TCWQC, you'll find stairways leading up to a cafe and other eateries, on the other side of the creekside condos.

Maple Leaf Community Garden (25 steps up and down): Head back to the *Wiggle Posts* sculpture at the downstream end of the channel. From there, cross 5th Avenue NE using the south crosswalk, and walk east a half block on NE 103rd to the Maple Leaf Community Garden (8).

This 0.4-acre hillside park is a multifunctional neighborhood hangout, playground, and P-Patch community gardens site. The property was bought by the city in 2003, and the gardens were opened in 2007. First you'll step up a short, colorfully tiled stairway to a circular toolshed. **WWW** The shed has the rounded waviness of adobe, with a cone-shaped roof lending a kind of madcap Disneyland effect.

Turn left at the shed, and walk beside some of the garden plots until you reach a set of stone steps. These lead up to the labyrinth and viewpoint that occupies the farthest, highest corner of the garden. **WWW** The labyrinth is child-proportioned, perhaps a dozen feet across, etched into concrete and surrounded by a low circular stone wall. Sitting on the wall, you'll see garden plots, tall tree snags towering above the slope to attract woodpeckers, and colorful sculptures dotting the hillside here and there.

To the NE 97th Street Stairs (29 steps down): From the garden you'll be doing a bit of zigzagging before you reach the next couple of sets of stairs and the end of your walk. Exit the garden to the right, and walk east along NE 103rd Street for a block and a half, when you'll carefully cross the arterial Roosevelt Way NE.

One block after crossing Roosevelt, turn right onto 12th Avenue NE. Walk south on 12th for five blocks, then turn left onto NE 96th Street, walking east. After one block, carefully cross busy 15th Avenue NE. Continue east about halfway down the block, where the street abruptly dead-ends, and take the narrow walkway on the left marked by a timber side-rail. The walkway leads downhill about 100 feet until the street picks up again; a few steps after, turn left onto 17th Avenue NE.

Walk north for one block on 17th. Then turn right onto NE 97th Street and walk east another block. Here, the street right-of-way turns 90 degrees to the left and continues as 19th Avenue NE. Here at the turn, you'll find the top of the recently renovated NE 97th Street stairs (9).

To the NE 95th Street Stairs (108 steps down): After reaching the bottom of the NE 97th Street stairs, continue straight on the dirt path toward 20th Avenue NE, then turn right. Walk south on 20th, first past a handful of houses and then past Sacajawea Elementary School. On the left watch for the

ENGINEERING URBAN NATURE

Until recently, TCWQC was an overflow parking lot for Northgate Mall. The South Fork of Thornton Creek, which originates just a few hundred yards northwest across I-5, ran in pipes beneath the asphalt. During heavy rains, runoff from the freeway, the Northgate Mall parking lot, and surrounding streets and yards filled the pipes and cascaded swiftly downstream. Heavy flows were common in the downstream parts of Thornton Creek, scouring away the streambed gravel that's essential to fish life.

In September 2009, the creek was daylighted via the 2.7-acre ravine that now makes up the Thornton Creek Water Quality Channel. Even with the new condo complex, this redevelopment reduced the impervious surface area of the old parking lot by almost 80 percent. A necklace of ponds, channels, and plantings mimics the way natural drainages work, filtering the creek and slowing it down when rains are heavy. Theoretically, this makes the creek more hospitable for life downstream, because it flows cleaner, slower, and year-round.

The channel also looks and functions like an elaborate public sunken garden filled with ponds, plantings, a babbling brook, and modern art and sculpture. Midway around the sidewalk loop encircling the channel (7), there's a 64-step staircase leading up to NE 100th Street WWW, with nice views from the top.

street sign indicating the NE 95th Street right-of-way, which marks a walkway leading to a flight of stairs (10).

Toward the bottom of the steps, as busy Lake City Way comes into view, the 95th Street stairs turn sharply to the left to make a final descent to the street. At the bottom you'll find a lighted crosswalk, which will conveniently and safely lead you across Lake City Way.

After crossing, you'll have a choice: you can turn left and walk up Lake City Way to your starting point at NE 98th Street, or you can walk ahead a few steps and then turn left onto Ravenna Avenue NE. Both routes are roughly parallel, but Lake City Way has the advantage of a sidewalk the whole way. It's also very busy and noisy. Ravenna is more pleasant, but you'll need to be vigilant about cars: the road has no sidewalk to speak of initially, though a sidewalk does appear about midway to NE 98th.

Whichever route you choose, head north until you reach NE 98th Street and the starting/ending point of your walk. From this point a side trip to Meadowbrook Pond is convenient by car. It's another stormwater management project that doubles as a giant art installation and wildlife refuge. WWW

Down the 95th Street stairs, Maple Leaf

6 Laurelhurst

Until 150 years ago, Laurelhurst was a heavily wooded peninsula jutting into a pristine bay. For the local Puget Salish people, it was a seasonal fishing camp, but for the balance of the year, it was probably pretty quiet here. That all changed in the 1890s when Yesler Town and its wood mill were built, just off the western side of the peninsula. The mill swiftly consumed the old-growth forest, clearing the way for a new era of development. Today Laurelhurst is a neighborhood of carefully landscaped homes, with constantly changing views of Union Bay and Lake Washington from its winding, hilly streets.

As you walk the streets and stairways, you might imagine the industrial sounds of the mill, or the *thwack* of a ball being struck on Seattle's first golf course, laid out about the same time as Yesler Town. These were the first events in the peninsula's rapid transformation. By 1910, just two decades after the mill arrived, Laurelhurst had twenty homes. It was still isolated by water and rough terrain, but its direction was set. It became the affluent neighborhood where Bill Gates Jr. grew up, and where Senators Warren G. Magnuson and Daniel J. Evans retired. It's very family-oriented, too: the percentage of households with kids is twice that of Seattle as a whole. Many residents who grew up here have returned to raise families of their own.

Along the walk you'll explore a lengthy, scenic stairway down to the Laurelhurst Beach Club. You'll discover a hidden stairway just off someone's driveway, dropping into a shadowy arbor on the way to streets below. Another very discreet stairway takes you to the street-end site of one of the commercial launch landings that tied Laurelhurst to Seattle in the early 1900s.

Do the walk in April, and you stand a great chance of finding the neighborhood in full flower, the air saturated with perfume.

Length:	**1.9 miles**
Walking Time:	1 hour 15 minutes
Steps Down:	222
Steps Up:	101
Kid-Friendly:	This is a short, fairly easy walk, mostly down. Laurelhurst Playfield/Community Center, at the start, offers a playground and restrooms (see www.seattle.gov/parks/centers/laurelcc.htm). Nearby Union Bay Natural Area WWW is another open, scenic place where kids can frolic and the family can picnic.
Cafes/Pubs:	Nearby University Village and Sand Point Way, directly to the north, offer many choices. If you pack a lunch, Laurelhurst Playfield and Union Bay Natural Area are great places to picnic.

Getting There: Park in the lot at Laurelhurst Playfield/Community Center at 4554 NE 41st Street (restrooms available when the center is open). Metro Transit Route 25 runs between Downtown and Laurelhurst via Eastlake, Portage Bay, and the U District, and stops right at the beginning of the walk, at the SE corner of Laurelhurst Playfield (48th Avenue NE and NE 41st Street).

To the "Hidden Stairs" (61 steps down): From your start at Laurelhurst Playfield/Community Center, walk east along NE 41st Street, with glimpses of Lake Washington ahead. The streets intersect at crazy angles here, but all you

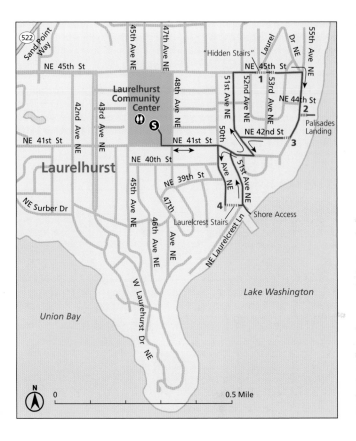

have to know is that once you pass 50th Avenue NE, take the next left, onto 51st Avenue NE. From here, you'll be heading up a fairly steep uphill grade past well-tended homes until 51st Avenue comes to an end. This marks a T junction with NE 45th Street.

At the T turn right and walk east along NE 45th. Here it's time to look for landmarks that point out the elusive "Hidden Stairs." Where NE 45th starts bending left, watch for a sign indicating the junction of NE 45th Street and 52nd Avenue NE. Just before the sign, look for a sidewalk that curves down and away from the street, running briefly alongside a driveway. That sidewalk **WWW** will bring you to a hidden stairway that descends 34 steps through a leafy laurel tunnel (1).

At the bottom of the stairway, take care as you cross 53rd Avenue NE to the next set of stairs. After just 27 steps, the grade once again becomes gentle enough for a real street. Continue downhill on NE 45th Street, with views of Kirkland across the lake. **WWW** At the bottom, cross 55th Avenue NE, turning right to walk along the far (eastern) side of 55th.

To Palisades Landing (67 steps down): Walk south on the lake side of 55th Avenue NE. Then, as 55th begins a gentle curve to the right, look for a street sign on the right indicating NE 43rd Street. Just opposite the sign, you'll find a stairway on your side of the street. Take these stairs, which end in a broad pathway past an enormous sequoia tree **WWW**, to a sweet lakeside overview (2). **WWW** You're visiting one of Seattle's 149 public shoreline street-ends, maintained

Looking back up the Laurelcrest stairs

under a special city program. (For more information, search online for "SDOT Street Ends.")

In the early 1900s this site, known as Palisades Landing, was used by a commercial launch to transport passengers between the eastern peninsula and Madison Park. Using this and two landings on the western side of the peninsula, these launches were the primary city connection for an isolated neighborhood. The pilings you see here are actually what remains of a later pier (not the original launch pier) built farther out after Lake Washington receded in 1917. Today this street-end is a peaceful public refuge for lakeside viewing, though it's encroached upon by private landowners, as are many of the shoreline street-ends throughout Seattle.

To the NE 42nd Street Stairs (101 steps up): To continue your stairway walk, climb back up from Palisades Landing (2) and to the street, turning left at the top of the stairs. Continue down the lake side of 55th Avenue NE until you see the sign for NE 42nd across the street—and your next stairs (3). Carefully cross over and head up 34 more stairs, continuing ahead on NE 42nd Street once you reach the top.

To the Laurelcrest Stairs (94 steps down): Once on NE 42nd Street, you'll be twisting and turning from one street to another in order to reach your next stairway. Here you'll start recognizing some of the streets you've covered before. From NE 42nd Street take the next left at 51st Avenue NE, which you traversed in the opposite direction earlier. Turn right at the next block, NE 41st Street. Heading west along NE 41st Street, you'll quickly pass Latimer Place and 51st Avenue NE on your left. Turn left at the next street, 50th Avenue NE. Walk south down this street almost to its end, where you'll see a stairway railing on the left side of the street—the top of the Laurelcrest stairs (4).

As you go down these steps, you'll have views of Lake Washington as well as fleeting glimpses of adjoining residences. **WWW** This stairway seems quiet and unassuming, yet graceful in shape and proportion, as it curves down toward the lake. The elegant stairway lamps complete the picture.

At the bottom the mood shifts a bit, as you find yourself in an open paved area with parking spaces to the right. To reach the lake, walk alongside the fence on the right, which separates the public access area from the Laurelhurst Beach Club (open from late spring to early fall for neighborhood residents). To get a lakeside view, pick your way between the parking barrier and the fence.

To return to your starting point, walk uphill on 51st Avenue NE. Turn left at NE 41st Street and continue west to Laurelhurst Playfield/ Community Center at 48th Avenue NE, on the right near the top of the hill.

From Laurelhurst Playfield, an additional route explores the western side of the peninsula and Union Bay Natural Area. **WWW**

7 University of Washington

The discreet and verdant Fluke Hall stairs

This jaunt takes you to outlying areas and hidden gems on the University of Washington campus, without neglecting the better-known sites like Red Square and Rainier Vista. A stairway walk can be incredibly exciting here in early April, when you're most likely to catch the Yoshino cherry trees in extravagant bloom all around the Quad. You'll tread the Wahkiakum Lane stairs, which we consider the grandest stairway on campus, but you'll also see many off-the-wall tidbits like the "Stairs to Nowhere," the odd little gargoyles peering down from Collegiate Gothic buildings, or the surrealist art installation otherwise known as the Sylvan Theater.

The route crisscrosses the beautiful UW campus and even takes a brief foray onto nearby University Way NE, using a series of stairways and a footbridge to get there. You'll have a chance to check out the eateries and hangouts on "The Ave" or visit University Book Store—a great place for book-browsing.

You'll view abundant art and architecture all along the way, and get to know some of the fascinating history of this 150-year-old institution, a Seattle neighborhood in its own right.

Length:	**2.6 miles (2 miles without a stroll up and down The Ave)**
Walking Time:	1 hour 30 minutes (1 hour without The Ave)
Steps Down:	273
Steps Up:	325
Kid-Friendly:	Not especially kid-oriented, but it's short, with lots of facilities.
Cafes/Pubs:	You'll find lots of eateries of multiple ethnic persuasions on The Ave, as well as a brewery and alehouse.

Getting There: This walk begins and ends in the University of Washington's huge E1 parking lot, just off the east side of Montlake Boulevard, north of the stadium. On major event days consider alternative walks nearby, like walk 6 "Laurelhurst." Otherwise, weekend parking in E1 is free and plentiful, from noon Saturday to 6 AM Monday. On Saturday before noon you'll be charged $6/day at the automated E1 gate; weekdays it's $15. If you're paying to park, go to a manned gatehouse (search online "UW parking rates" for current rates and gatehouse locations). There, you can pay the daily fee and return for a prorated refund later, for any time less than 4 hours.

If you're taking the bus, several Metro Transit routes stop along NE 45th Street near University Village and parking lot E1. MT25 runs weekdays only between Laurelhurst and Downtown; MT65 runs between Lake City and Wedgwood, and MT75 goes from the U District north to Lake City.

The North "Twin Stairs" and "Dorm Stairs" (74 steps up): From the E1 parking lot, walk west toward Montlake Boulevard and the curving twin staircase about halfway between the north and south ends of the lot (1). The two stairways sweep up from opposing sides, joining in midair to form a footbridge over the busy boulevard. **WWW** They rest on a series of descending pylons, the final steps extending from the last pylon almost to the ground; a short length of wooden steps completes the journey. You'll start the walk here on these "North Stairs" and complete your loop on a very similar stairway at the south end of the lot.

After 29 steps, you'll be on the footbridge. From there you'll see a long set of stairs straight ahead, with a dorm towering on the hill beyond. First, cross the Burke-Gilman Trail at the far side of the bridge, looking both ways for speeding bicycles. **WWW**

You actually don't climb the entire length of the stairway ahead. After 45 steps and just before the top of the first flight, turn left onto a narrow asphalt path running between blackberry bushes and other shrubs. This path runs a short distance south, curving gradually up to a sidewalk next to Mason Road.

To the Fluke Hall Stairs and the "Mayan Wall" (94 steps up): Walk south beside Mason Road, with the multilevel Padelford Parking Garage across the street on your right. Just past it, you'll see a pyramidal bicycle shelter on the right, in front of Fluke Hall. It's right at the base of the Wahkiakum Lane stairs that quickly disappear up the hill. You'll be coming down these stairs on the return part of your loop.

As you draw abreast of the pyramidal bicycle shelter, the sidewalk ends, but a crosswalk will take you over to the west side of Mason Road. You can pick up a sidewalk and continue in the same direction. Just beyond Fluke Hall turn right, into a small parking lot (N24) next to a loading dock. Tucked discreetly behind the lot and away from the street sits one of our favorite stairways on campus (2). Brilliant silvery handrails and slender lamp posts weave up an elegantly planted slope, a gorgeous setting for these out-of-the-way stairs.

There are 39 steps to your first landing. Ignoring the sidewalk to the right, continue up the stairs. After another 28 steps there's another walkway heading off to the right, a digression that's worth a quick look. Just a few feet along, you'll find a retaining wall that moonlights as a work of art. The gray cinder-block structure looks like the side of a squat Mayan pyramid, each rank of bricks set back a small, regular distance from the one below, with chunky benches emerging organically out of the base. **WWW** Farther up the path is a little P-Patch garden nestling against Fluke Hall and a bit beyond that, the walkway intersects with the Wahkiakum stairs, mentioned before.

Save those stairs for later, and return to your junction. Walk up the last 27 steps leading to a walkway that intersects E Stevens Way NE.

To the Sylvan Columns and Amphitheater Stairs (26 steps up, 26 steps down): Across Stevens Way is the brand-new Husky Union Building (HUB). Turn left onto the sidewalk along Stevens, next to the Facilities Services Administration Building. You'll pass two roads on the left, Jefferson Road and then Benton Lane. Just past Benton, look for a crosswalk leading across Stevens Way toward the Paul Allen Center. After crossing, turn left onto the sidewalk.

Just past a delivery driveway that slopes down into the Paul Allen Center, two asphalt walkways diverge to the right from the sidewalk. The first follows the wall of the Paul Allen Center and toward the Drumheller Fountain (4), visible through the trees if it's running.

Step onto the second asphalt walkway, which angles away from the sidewalk and through some undergrowth before it opens onto a wide grassy amphitheater surrounded by trees. You've entered the Sylvan Theater **WWW**, an island of tranquility on campus (3).

Inside the ring of trees is an elevated stage area, with two surreally isolated stairways curving up both sides in 6 quick steps. Four Ionic columns tower

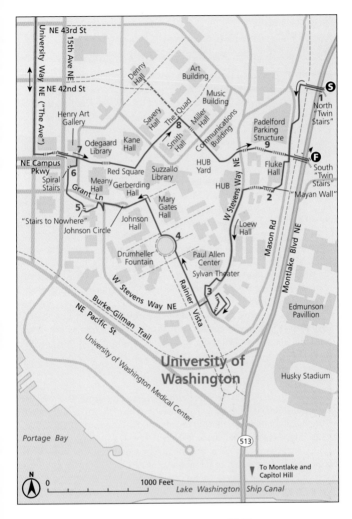

behind the stage, supporting nothing in particular. **WWW** The columns, made of hand-carved cedar, once supported the portico of the original university building where the Fairmont Olympic Hotel stands today, at the corner of University and 4th (see walk 15, "Downtown").

UW ICONS: RAINIER VISTA AND DRUMHELLER FOUNTAIN

In 1907 the Olmsted Brothers firm was commissioned to design landscaping for the 1909 Alaska-Yukon-Pacific Exposition on the UW campus. John C. Olmsted must have visited on a day when Mount Rainier was visible, because he designed the grounds to frame a stunning view of Rainier, 60 miles away. Under his plan, the main axis of the Exposition became a broad mall known as Rainier Vista. He pointed it directly at the mountain, leaving tall conifers in place to frame the view.

The buildings surrounding Drumheller Fountain are not the ones designed for the 1909 Exposition, which were only temporary. `WWW` The fountain is different too, in both name and plumbing. In 1909 it was called Geyser Basin, and had only a small center fountain. Today, north of the basin, a broad asphalt walkway rises between Mary Gates Hall and Johnson Hall up to Red Square. In 1909 this walkway space contained a series of gentle water cascades stepping down almost to Geyser Basin.

After the Exposition the fountain was dismantled and the cascades were filled in, but the circular pond remained. It was used, among other things, as the field of battle for logrolling contests put on by the nearby College of Forestry. Then in 1961 UW Regent Joseph Drumheller donated a much larger fountain, with a center jet that can launch water 100 feet into the air. Hopefully, you'll be lucky enough to visit when it's going full blast.

On the opposite side of the theater from where you entered, another walkway guides you around the stage area. From here, look up to the Sylvan Columns for a fifth, "bonus" column standing in their midst. This apparent Sylvan sibling is actually a power plant smokestack, two blocks away.

Back at the street, you're now at the intersection of Stevens Way and NE Mason Road. Head across to the northeast corner, and continue east on the sidewalk next to Mason Road.

After maybe 15 yards, turn up a sidewalk that takes you toward the "MUELLER HALL" sign. Just ahead and slightly to the left, you'll see a grassy sunken bowl, with stairways on either side, descending to the courtyard at the heart of Mueller Hall. `WWW`

Head down the 26 south-side stairs to view this unusual "daylight basement" building, which houses part of the UW Materials Science and Engineering Department. The low-profile 1989 design allows the older Roberts Hall (1921), just to the east, to retain pride of place along Stevens Way.

Step up the north-side stairs to ground level, then turn right to follow the plaza that forms the roof of Mueller Hall. As you turn back toward Mason Road and the sidewalk you came in on, you'll pass the magnificent Gothic-style Roberts Hall on your left. A close look at the sculpted cartouche above the door shows a man with a mining pick—a hint of this building's previous life as host to UW's former College of Mines.

To Rainier Vista and Drumheller Fountain: Back at Mason Road, retrace your steps to the corner of Mason and Stevens Way NE. From the corner, first cross left over Mason at the crosswalk and then a few steps ahead take another crosswalk over Stevens. This puts you in front of a gravel walkway looking up Rainier Vista toward your next destination, Drumheller Fountain. Before you head that way, check out the grand view from the monument located slightly up Stevens Way, in the middle of the Vista.

From Stevens Way, start walking up Rainier Vista, a broad avenue designed to frame the view of Mount Rainier, 60 miles southeast. The conifer-lined view can be spectacular, especially with the spouting fountain positioned in the foreground. Combine that with blooming Yoshino cherry trees in the springtime, and for a few years at least, it's a triple-threat photo opportunity. (Once the light-rail station opens at Husky Stadium, Rainier Vista will be carrying more foot and bicycle traffic, so UW planners are working on modifications that entail loss of the cherry trees along south Rainier Vista.)

When you reach Drumheller Fountain (4), look for the nearby sundial sitting in front of a flower patch. It was created as a memorial gift by the class of 1912, and has moved around campus quite a bit across the years. Unfortunately, the dial is off a few degrees, so it won't give you an accurate time.

Finding the "Stairs to Nowhere" (13 steps up, 23 steps down): Stroll around the large circle of Drumheller Fountain (4), then continue along the Rainier Vista axis, following the broad asphalt walkway between Mary Gates and Johnson halls. Just past those two buildings and well before the stairs leading up to Red Square, turn left onto a brick-paved walkway. It'll take you past Gerberding Hall on the right, to a traffic circle at the end of Grant Lane (Johnson Circle). Follow the left-hand side of the circle out to the intersection of Grant Place with W Stevens Way NE, which runs off to the left. Cross Stevens and just a few feet along the sidewalk, turn left down a small 10-step stairway. At the bottom follow the sidewalk to the right, next to the beautiful, stately Architecture Hall (look up!).

The sidewalk takes a couple of twists and turns between the Architecture Hall and a low-slung wooden building, one of the Guthrie Annex buildings. You'll eventually round a corner of the annex building to be confronted by the "Stairs to Nowhere" (5). There are 13 steps up and back down—the stairs literally go nowhere.

These stairs were an architecture student project, completed in 1988. A team of grads and final-year undergrads designed it, fabricated the trusses in the school's shop, and created the framing on site. The result is a whimsical yet sleekly beautiful place for students to gather.

To the "Spiral Stairs" (53 steps up): From the "Stairs to Nowhere" (5), follow the sidewalk downhill to the intersection of Grant Lane and 15th Avenue NE, visible up ahead. Cross at the intersection and walk north up 15th, on the east side of the street. Ahead you'll see a cylindrical structure—the "Spiral Stairs" (6).

Spiral up the stairs to a plaza on the next level. From there, make a left at the first opportunity. You'll be walking between a row of three pyramidal glass-and-steel sculptures on the left paired with three rectangular boxes on the right—perhaps light boxes for the level below. As you approach the entrance to the Henry Art Gallery (7), turn left again and head toward the footbridge that crosses 15th Avenue NE.

A Taste of "The Ave" (39 steps up, 39 steps down): The next part of the route takes you on a quick visit to University Way NE, better known as "The Ave." It's a busy hangout for UW students, with lots of food places. The University Book Store is another fun place to spend time and money.

This is an out-and-in section of the walk, free of stairways, which returns to the Henry Art Gallery entrance area (7) via the footbridge. You can skip The Ave section, and just continue the walk starting from where the Henry Art Gallery is mentioned in the next section.

On the main route, cross the 15th Avenue footbridge heading west. Take the steps down from the bridge itself and then some more steps from Schmitz Hall Plaza down to the street. Walk west for one block alongside NE Campus Parkway, then turn right onto University Way NE. Just past NE 41st Street you'll be in the thick of The Ave with all its eateries.

Once you reach NE 43rd Street, cross The Ave to return along the west side—unless you want to look in on the University Book Store, just a couple of doors farther up on the east side.

On the way back, after you cross NE 42nd Street and pass Big Time Brewery and Alehouse, start looking for a crosswalk that will take you back over to the east side of The Ave. Keep walking south on The Ave until you reach NE Campus Parkway, then turn left to retrace your steps up and over the footbridge.

When you reach the first landing of the bridge steps, notice the sculpture, *Dancer with Flat Hat*, by Phillip Levine. He is one of the Northwest's leading sculptors, with more than thirty works installed in public spaces. He is known for his representation of the human figure, in an era dominated by abstract sculpture. One of Levine's works, *Walking on Logs*, greets tens of thousands of motorists each day as they drive in and out of West Seattle.

From Red Square to the Quad (26 steps up): Cross the footbridge back over 15th and continue ahead, past the Henry Art Gallery entrance (7), toward the tall George Washington statue and into Red Square.

The George Washington statue, by Chicago sculptor Lorado Taft, was installed at the entrance to the 1909 Exposition near its place today. Its permanent 24-foot-tall base was built thirty years later by the Works Progress Administration, during the Depression.

From the statue, look left to see a modern work, Robert Irwin's *9 Spaces 9 Trees*. It may look like an outdoor seating area surrounded by a high mesh fence, but look closely and you'll see it's actually nine trees in large planters, each in its own self-contained grid space. It was originally commissioned in 1980 for the rooftop of a building elsewhere, but was reimagined and re-created here in 2007.

Now walk ahead and up two flights of steps, 20 in all, to find yourself at the edge of brick-paved Red Square. The glorious Tudor Collegiate Gothic edifice of Suzzallo Library stands straight ahead, with the "campanile" directly to your left. The campanile doesn't house traditional campus bells, but provides ventilation for the five-level parking garage under your feet. Just ahead of the campanile on the left, you'll see the strong vertical supports and tall rectangular window spaces that mark Kane Hall. Walk across the square toward a point just between Kane Hall and Suzzallo Library.

There you'll approach Barnett Newman's 1967 *Broken Obelisk* sculpture, one of several copies of this work. Newman is better known as a painter; this is considered the best-known of his six sculptures. In the politically tempestuous year of 1968, Newman moved another copy of this sculpture out of Washington, DC, after critics compared it to a broken, upside-down Washington Monument.

Pass to the right around *Broken Obelisk*, walking between Kane Hall and Suzzallo Library straight ahead onto Pierce Lane. A few steps later you'll cross Spokane Lane, and then you'll step up two sets of triple stairs and into the Liberal Arts Quadrangle, or "the Quad" (8).

The Quad is a campus magnet in spring, when the Yoshino cherry trees bloom all around the perimeter. If you visit then, you'll witness how effectively their pink billows soften the edges of the surrounding Collegiate Gothic façades while complementing their subtle brick and terra-cotta hues.

On some of the buildings unusual gargoyle figures hunker at the base of the gables, looking down on passersby. For Smith Hall on the southwest corner of the Quad, sculptor Dudley Pratt created twenty-eight of these figures in 1940, when the structure was built. Two groups on the north side of Smith Hall depict Seattle history; other figures on the northwest corner of the building, where you entered the Quad, memorialize World War I and other international themes. You can see more figures on the southeast side of Smith Hall when you exit the Quad as well as gargoyles by other artists on other buildings, particularly on Miller and Savery halls.

One last attraction, Denny Hall, is just a stone's throw from the Quad. Denny Hall was the first structure built when the university moved here from its original location downtown. It's a magnificent French Renaissance building constructed of Olympia-area (Tenino) sandstone, with conical turrets, deep gables, and steeply pitched slate roofs. It was opened for use in 1895, is still in use, and is also one of the most photographed buildings on campus. To see Denny Hall, just take the broad path from the middle of the Quad north, passing out of the Quad into a wide, newish plaza area. You'll see it looming straight ahead.

From the Quad to the Wahkiakum Lane Stairs (185 steps down): To exit the Quad (8) and continue with the route, take the sidewalk from the middle of the Quad south, in the opposite direction from Denny Hall. This pathway, otherwise known as King Lane, takes you out of the Quad between Smith Hall on the right and Miller Hall on the left. After a short set of 15 steps down, you'll cross Skagit Lane, continuing ahead with Thomson Hall on your left and Grieg Garden on your right.

Take a quick peek into Grieg Garden, especially in early spring when the azaleas and rhododendrons are in bloom. A couple of decades ago this was a parking lot, but now it's a quiet space surrounded by mature trees and shrubs. It's anchored by an imposing statue of Norwegian composer Edvard Grieg, created for the 1909 Exposition.

Once you've nearly passed Thomson Hall on your left, watch for two sturdy gateposts topped by lamps. As you pass between them, you'll see two paths; turn right onto the narrower asphalt sidewalk that curves downhill away from Thomson Hall. The path curves down toward a parking lot (N22) on your left, entering it as a marked crosswalk. Follow the crosswalk safely through the parking lot toward the street ahead, E Stevens Way NE. Take the crosswalk you'll find there to the other side of Stevens, where you'll be met by the top of a stairway and a sign: "STAIRS TO MONTLAKE PARKING AREA."

Follow these stairs, initially with Padelford Hall on the left and Hall Health Center on the right. You're now on Wahkiakum Lane, a wonderful stairway interspersed with sections of path (9). Take it all the way down to Mason Road, passing the familiar pyramidal bicycle parking shelter at the bottom, on your left.

At Mason, take the crosswalk straight ahead, to a short stairway of 16 steps. At the bottom of these is the Burke-Gilman Trail. Carefully cross, watching

for speeding bicyclists as before. Now you're crossing to your starting place at parking lot E1, this time on the southernmost of the two footbridges over Montlake Boulevard. At the far end of the bridge take one of the twin stairways down to the asphalt (1). That's 25 steps on the left, 28 on the right—your choice!

PART II

CENTRAL SEATTLE

8   Madrona and Leschi

A distinctive stretch of stair-rich neighborhoods lies along the western shore of Lake Washington, between the SR 520 and I-90 bridges. Here, the bluff above the lake is creased by deep ravines, harboring Olmsted-designed parks and beautiful homes. In some places residents combined private with government resources to buy undeveloped hillside acreage, then worked to restore it as accessible greenspace.

The neighborhoods running north–south from the 520 bridge include Madison Park, Washington Park, Harrison/Denny Blaine, Madrona, and Leschi. Of these, Madrona is an especially rich vein of stairway treasure, with stairs discreetly linking streets that can't always make it completely down steep hills and across ravines. The neighborhood includes two of the premier open spaces in Seattle: Madrona Woods and the Leschi Natural Area. In addition to all the attractions on this route, there are many other wonderful stairs, views, and quiet greenspaces to discover here.

Length:	**1.7 miles (add 0.5 mile with optional route via James stairs)**
Walking Time:	1 hour 15 minutes (add 15 minutes with optional route via James stairs)
Steps Down:	371
Steps Up:	299 (add 106 for optional James stairs)
Kid-Friendly:	Madrona Playground is located near the start, with restrooms; Madrona Eatery and Ale House is a family favorite in the 'hood. All of these are on or near 34th Avenue, near the start.
Cafes/Pubs:	Aside from the Madrona Eatery and Ale House, near the start you'll also find the Hi Spot Cafe, Madrona Market and Deli, two parks at either end for picnicking, and several other places where you can grab coffee or a snack.

Getting There: You'll start and end this walk near the small commercial beating heart of Madrona, which runs along 34th Avenue between E Spring and E Pike streets. If you're driving, park one street over in the residential

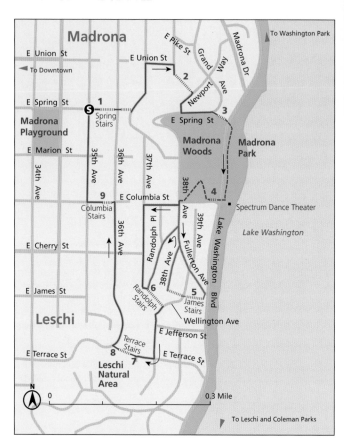

area, near the corner of 35th Avenue and E Spring Street. Metro Transit Route 2 conveniently stops at 34th and E Union Street (one block from Spring), coming all the way from West Queen Anne via Seattle Center, Downtown, and First Hill. MT3 stops at 34th and both Spring and Union, arriving from East Queen Anne via Seattle Center, Downtown, and First Hill; you can also take MT3 north to Madrona, from Center Park (near Rainier Avenue and MLK Boulevard) and Judkins Park.

To the Spring Street Stairs (88 steps down): From 35th and E Spring Street, next to St. Therese School, head down a cobblestone cul-de-sac ending

A twisting section of the Spring Street stairs

in a flight of stairs (1). You'll descend two brief flights with a ramp between them, ending at 36th Avenue. Cross 36th and continue down another 64 steps to 37th Avenue. At the bottom of the steps is a tree-filled ravine. Turn left onto 37th Avenue.

To the 38th Avenue Stairs (137 steps down): As you follow along 37th, the street makes a bit of a dogleg before reaching E Union Street. Turn right onto Union, noting the ramp and stairway heading up the hill in the opposite direction—another road not taken in this stairway-rich area! Walk one block downhill on Union until it stops at 38th Avenue. Turn right onto 38th, marked by a "DEAD END" sign. The 38th Avenue stairs (2) are just ahead of you where the street dead-ends. These 137 steps take you down to Newport Way.

Turn right onto Newport Way and continue a few yards to a T intersection. At this point a trail leads into Madrona Woods, straight ahead of you. Stay on the pavement, turning left onto E Spring Street, and head downhill along the north edge of Madrona Woods.

After a couple of dozen yards look for a street sign on the right indicating Grand Avenue, heading uphill to the left. Here Spring morphs into a path and stairway leading toward Lake Washington (3). Continue down this path, ignoring the footbridge on the right (it leads into Madrona Woods, which you'll enter later from below). Flowing down the ravine on your right is a spring-fed creek, recently daylighted by a coalition of Seattle Parks and Friends of Madrona Woods. Their website, www.madronawoods.org, has extensive information and a great trail map.

Madrona Park (21 steps down): Toward the bottom of the slope, you'll step down a short stairway to Lake Washington Boulevard. Cross the boulevard into Madrona Park, which fronts the shore. As you face the lake, you'll see an extensive area where shoreline salmon habitat has been restored and replanted. Turn right and walk south through the park. You can take a path through the restored area, or stick closer to Lake Washington Boulevard. You'll pass some restrooms before reaching the old Madrona Park Bathhouse, now the practice and performance space for Donald Byrd's Spectrum Dance Theater.

MADRONA PARK HISTORY

In 1908 the City of Seattle bought over 12 acres from Seattle Electric Company, which had run an electric trolley line to Madrona in 1891 as the first step in developing the neighborhood. The plan was to create Madrona Park, in accord with John C. Olmsted's original vision for a park-laced boulevard running all the way from the shores of Lake Washington to Puget Sound. In 1928 the road from Montlake Bridge to Seward Park was renamed Lake Washington Boulevard, replacing a variety of other names for different portions of the road.

The first version of the Madrona Park Bathhouse was built in 1919. During the New Deal in the 1930s, the WPA built two floating docks offshore, which are still used by swimmers today. **WWW** Originally, one dock was used by black swimmers, the other by white. The story goes that in the 1950s, black swimmers began using both rafts, a small-scale act of integration that paved the way for the rest of the park's public facilities.

Madrona Woods (127 steps up): At the bathhouse, take the crosswalk back over Lake Washington Boulevard. Then head up timber stairs into the south side of Madrona Woods (4). WWW There are multiple sets of timber pathway steps on your route through the woods, although most of the way you'll be walking up a gravel path.

Turn left at the first two forks in the path, generally aiming for the southwest corner of the park. However, near the top look for a short flight of timber stairs heading up to the right. Take these, then immediately turn left again at the top. From here, the path heads directly south, following the slope. Soon it approaches a house, where it turns 90 degrees to the right, skirting the residence before coming out onto 38th Avenue and E Columbia Street.

At this point, if you'd like to check out another stairway, adding 106 stairs up and 15 minutes to this walk, follow the directions in the alternate route, "Option: James Stairs." This loop starts here and returns to the main route at the Randolph stairs (6), bypassing E Columbia Street and 37th Avenue. To continue with the main route, jump down to the next section, "To the Randolph stairs."

Option: James Stairs (106 stairs up)

To add the James stairs loop to your walk, exit Madrona Woods to the left along 38th Avenue. Curving gradually downhill to the left, 38th Avenue offers some nice views toward the lake.

You'll encounter two forks along the way. In both cases take the left fork, first away from Norwood Place and then away from 38th Avenue itself, onto Fullerton Avenue. Walk down Fullerton past the intersection with Wellington Avenue until you reach Lake Washington Boulevard, and you'll see a stairway heading uphill (5). WWW

The initial flight of the James stairs ends at Wellington. Cross Wellington and continue up the stairs just beyond, until the stairs end at 38th Avenue. Turn right onto 38th and continue to Norwood Place, turning left. Norwood Place soon merges with Randolph Place, coming in from the right.

Continue south on Randolph Place until it makes a sudden hairpin turn to the right and uphill. Around the corner the street becomes 37th Avenue, the incoming route of the main walk. At this point you'll see a sign indicating that Randolph Place continues as a stairway down the ravine. Rejoin the main route here, taking the Randolph stairs down, and continue with the main walk at "To the Terrace Stairs." ♦

To the Randolph Stairs (125 steps down): As you exit Madrona Woods on the main route, cross 38th Avenue and walk west on E Columbia Street past Randolph Place on your left, to 37th Avenue. Farther ahead you can see a portion of the Columbia stairs, part of which you'll explore later on. For now, turn left onto 37th Avenue.

Polished entrance stones at the Leschi Natural Area

Follow 37th Avenue uphill, heading south; soon 37th Avenue crests and starts downhill, eventually making an abrupt hairpin turn to the left. At this turn you'll see a street sign on the outside of the curve, marking the head of your next stairway (6). **WWW** The Randolph Place right-of-way here is actually a curving set of 125 stairs. **WWW** At the bottom, turn right.

To the Terrace Stairs (101 steps up): After coming down the Randolph stairs and turning right, continue uphill on Randolph Avenue. One block past Jefferson (which heads downhill toward Lake Washington), turn right onto E Terrace Street. After walking a few uphill yards, you'll arrive at the base of the Terrace stairs (7). **WWW**

Leschi Natural Area: About two-thirds of the way up the Terrace stairs, you'll see a path, marked by a handrail, that branches off to the left. This is an entrance to Leschi Natural Area, a community-organized and -maintained open space. Continue past this entrance all the way up the stairs, bearing slightly to the left at the top to get to the main entrance at 36th Avenue (8). Here in 3 scenic acres of wooded ravine, you can follow bark-covered paths through patches of Indian plum, snowberries, and sword fern, rest on big flat boulders, and enjoy open views of Mount Rainier and Lake Washington. **WWW**

To the Columbia Stairs and Walk's End (71 steps up): From Leschi Natural Area, walk north along 36th Avenue. Continue one block past E Cherry Street, to E Columbia Street. Here on the left, the Columbia Street right-of-way is a final staircase taking you up 71 stairs to 35th Avenue, near your starting point (9). But you don't have to end your walk here! Nearby attractions like Nora's Woods and the hidden walkway and footbridge just north of Madrona Drive are convenient and very much worth exploring. **WWW**

9 Eastlake, North Capitol Hill, and Portage Bay

Pausing on the Blaine stairs

This North Capitol Hill walk features two of the longest and arguably most scenic stairways in Seattle: the Blaine Street and Howe Street stairs. They run in parallel one block apart, down the west flank of Capitol Hill. In earlier days they connected one streetcar line on Eastlake Avenue at the base of Capitol Hill with a line running along the crown of the hill on 10th Avenue E. The stairs continue to be an essential part of the neighborhood, and they're constantly in use. You'll come across a lot of friendly locals out for a casual walk or a workout. We've even heard that firefighters from the nearby station sometimes climb the stairs in full gear!

This walk also explores one-of-a-kind neighborhood attractions like Streissguth Gardens. Located just off the Blaine stairs, the gardens are a refuge of carefully tended native plants and wandering paths, with views changing with the seasons (see "A Hidden Treasure"). Another attraction is the impressive Colonnade Mountain Bike Skills Park, which covers 2 acres of cavernous alcove beneath I-5, on the border of the Capitol Hill and Eastlake neighborhoods. Moving up and over Capitol Hill to Portage Bay, you'll discover a beautiful little shoreside park, hidden down a short flight of curving stairs. Everywhere on this walk you'll enjoy gorgeous views—of the Cascades, Lake Union and Portage Bay, and Queen Anne Hill.

Length:	**2.3 miles**
Walking Time:	2 hours
Steps Down:	349 (complete Howe stairs route adds 21)
Steps Up:	337 (complete Howe stairs route adds 195)
Kid-Friendly:	An abbreviated walk can be created by taking the Blaine stairs down to Colonnade Park and returning via the Howe stairs. Older kids might like an introduction to Colonnade Park, especially if they're into BMX or mountain biking.
Cafes/Pubs:	Coffee shops can be found off Eastlake and 10th avenues; see route description.

Getting There: Good on-street parking is available on 10th Avenue E between E Howe Street and E Blaine Street, where you'll be starting and ending your stroll. Keep an eye out for signs noting parking restrictions. If you're coming by bus, Metro Transit Route 49 stops on 10th and Howe, one block north of your starting point; it runs through Capitol Hill between Downtown and the University District.

Blaine Stairs (293 steps down): Look for a small cul-de-sac on E Blaine Street off the west side of 10th Avenue E. Your urban trailhead is right here, at the top of the Blaine stairs. About halfway down the first flight (1), a small path leads off to the left. This is one trailhead into Streissguth Gardens (there are other entrances below).

Continue down the Blaine stairs, which pick up again after you cross Broadway E. On the right, at the top of the next flight, sits one of the famous Sears catalog "kit houses" that were popular in Seattle in the early 1900s. **WWW**

Colonnade Mountain Bike Skills Park, Howe Stairs, and Roanoke Park (127 steps up, 16 steps down): The Blaine stairs end at Lakeview Boulevard E. Cross the street, entering Colonnade Mountain Bike Park beneath the tall columns of I-5 (2). This striking installation, consisting of more than a mile of trails spread across 2 acres, provides a smorgasbord of challenges to mountain bikers working on their skills. **WWW**

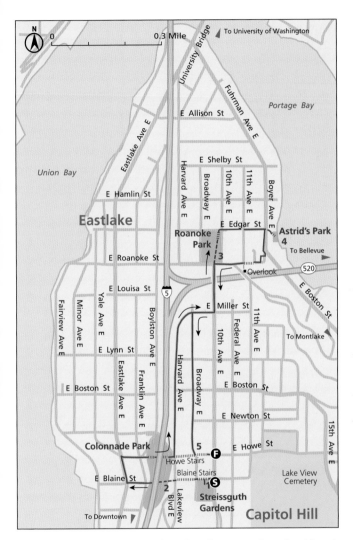

After crossing Lakeview into Colonnade Park, continue down the wide path under the freeway to the other side, where E Blaine Street resumes. Walk one block down Blaine to Eastlake Avenue E. To the left (south on Eastlake) is part of the Fred Hutchinson Cancer Research Center campus and a coffee shop, if

A HIDDEN TREASURE: STREISSGUTH GARDENS

There's a hidden but fully accessible urban retreat perched between busy, densely trafficked Capitol Hill above and Eastlake below. Back in 1972, Dan and Ann Streissguth bought two lots across the Blaine stairs from their own home (designed by Dan, an architect). Dan says there was no master plan to create these gardens; they just started pushing back a tangle of blackberry bushes, clematis, and horsetails on the new property, hardly realizing they were embarking on the project of a lifetime. As the garden grew and their vision for it expanded, the city bought adjacent land as greenspace. The Streissguths gifted their lots to create one large protected open space—with the proviso that they themselves maintain the plantings. The garden today is slightly larger than an acre, with paths intertwining on the side of the hill.

The garden's appearance is in flux with the seasons, which makes it worth visiting year round. Dan told us that his favorite time of the year is winter, when the views open up and the architecture of the trees and shrubs is revealed. You can learn more, or even volunteer, at www.streissguthgardens.com.

you're so inclined. To the right your walk continues north up Eastlake to the next street, E Howe Street. Turn right onto Howe and up a few stairs to reenter Colonnade Park at its north end. This stretch of the Howe stairs, approaching and crossing back under the freeway, has 106 stairs going up. WWW

Exit Colonnade Park at Lakeview Boulevard E. Use the crosswalk to get across Lakeview, noting the continuation of the Howe stairs straight ahead. You'll climb them on your return loop, but for now, turn to the left and step up 21 stairs to Harvard Avenue E. Here you're walking parallel to and above I-5, with great views of Lake Union, Queen Anne, and Gas Works Park. It's loud, but enjoy the view—you'll be walking away from the freeway soon enough.

Harvard runs parallel to the freeway for several blocks, then makes a gentle curve to the right where it becomes E Miller Street and starts to climb. Continue up E Miller to the stoplight at 10th Avenue E. Cross to the east side of 10th Avenue and then turn left, heading north along 10th. Note another coffee shop opportunity just a few steps along. Cross a bridge over SR 520, reaching a lighted crosswalk at E Roanoke Street. Cross over and enter Roanoke Park straight ahead (3). Head up the path along the east side of the park, until you reach a set of exit stairs in the northeast corner.

After stepping down the 16 exit stairs, cross 10th Avenue E, aiming for either side of the traffic barrier. This is the right-of-way for E Edgar Street, which the neighborhood maintains as open space. Sidewalks run down the hill on either side, with lovely views of Portage Bay and the Cascades beyond. WWW

Streissguth Gardens in April

After a block, E Edgar Street reasserts itself. Continue downhill on Edgar for two blocks until it ends at Boyer Avenue E. Cross to the other side of Boyer at the crosswalk.

Astrid's Park (40 steps up and down): Once you've crossed Boyer, turn right from the crosswalk, and almost before you take a step, you'll see a staircase to the left. Take it down 26 steps, then across a driveway to another brief flight of 14 stairs to Astrid's Park (4), a beautiful little pocket park built and maintained by volunteers. It's right at the edge of Portage Bay, with the docked boats of the Queen City Yacht Club in front of you and glimpses of houseboats beyond.

Return via the Howe Stairs Shortcut (170 steps up): After enjoying the views across the water, turn back up the stairs toward Boyer Avenue. Cross over and turn left, this time walking south along Boyer.

A few dozen feet along, the main street curves left while a narrow offshoot forks uphill to the right. Continue up the sidewalk on the right side of the small lane (confusingly also named Boyer). Soon this offshoot of E Boyer turns 90 degrees to the right, parallel to SR 520 running noisily above. A sign here shows the lane switching to E Roanoke Street, which continues uphill, passing a house on the right. Just about where E Roanoke peters out, you'll see another flight of stairs a few yards ahead on the left. At the top of the 14 stairs, turn right, up another 69 steps. Continue across 11th Avenue E to reach the sidewalk running along E Roanoke Street.

Last steps to Astrid's Park and Portage Bay

For a quick side visit, you can turn left at the top of the stairs and up a set of 9 broad slab steps to an overlook perched above SR 520, with broad views of Portage Bay and the Cascades. A marker is placed there in honor of Washington's pioneers of naturopathic and homeopathic medicine, including Herman Beardsley Bagley, who helped originate the plan for a ship canal linking Lake Washington with Puget Sound.

From the overlook, return to the head of the stairs you just came up and turn left, crossing 11th Avenue E to reach a sidewalk along E Roanoke.

Once you've reached the sidewalk next to E Roanoke and Roanoke Park (3), look for the far crosswalk that goes to the west side of 10th Avenue E. Cross Roanoke and then the SR 520 bridge, turning right at E Miller Street.

Retrace your steps down E Miller Street, then turn left at the next block, Broadway E. As you return to your starting spot, you'll be walking parallel to Harvard Avenue, one block up from I-5, through a quieter neighborhood of very lovely homes.

Your walk ends with a climb on the upper portion of the Howe stairs (5), ending at 10th Avenue E. This "Howe Stairs Shortcut," with 87 steps, is 195 steps shorter than the complete Howe stairs route described below. As you head up, note the interesting houses lining the way. Many have their own private walkways to the stairs. You'll eventually arrive at a small cul-de-sac that opens onto 10th Avenue E, and the end of your walk.

To complete the entire length of the Howe stairs, you can return from E Miller Street via Harvard Avenue E, retracing your original route next to I-5. Take the 21 steps down to Lakeview Boulevard where you immediately intersect the Howe stairs on your left. From there you can climb all 282 steps of this section of the Howe stairs. With the 106 steps under Colonnade Park you've already walked, you've covered all 388 steps—the longest stairway in Seattle!

10 East Queen Anne

This stairway walk is a fast-moving feast of outstanding views, classic early-1900s stairways, fascinating neighborhood history, and amazing art and architecture. Many of its more than 500 steps occur at the beginning, but the up front effort really pays off.

Conceptually, anyway, Galer Street transects Queen Anne east to west, dividing the north half of the hill from the south. The right-of-way begins from the shore of Lake Union and runs straight up and over the hill, passing near Queen Anne's highest point on its way to the far western side. In the real world, Galer "street" is mostly stairway as it climbs the eastern slope. You may have noticed these stairs while driving along Aurora Avenue under the Galer pedestrian overpass, and wondered where they go. On this walk you'll find out!

Queen Anne Avenue (the western reach of this walk) runs perpendicular to Galer, separating the east side of the hill from the west. Together, the two streets divide the hill into four quadrants. The next two stairway walks cover the southwest and northwest quadrants, respectively; this route wanders into both east-side quadrants, so we just call it the East Queen Anne walk. It starts from Westlake Marina and carries rapidly up the eastern flank of the hill, on a series of linked stairways. These first stairs offer beautiful views back toward Lake Union and Capitol Hill. Later, from higher vantage points, you'll even be able to peek over Capitol Hill for a glimpse of Lake Washington.

After making your way up the major part of the eastern slope, you'll turn south for an adventuresome little loop via Bhy Kracke Park, a hidden jewel with panoramic views of Lake Union, the Space Needle, and Downtown. Turning north from there, you'll pass the highest point on the hill as you approach the grand old 1909 Comstock stairs. This sweeping concrete stairway is right next to the commercial center of the neighborhood, yet it's tucked away from street view, top and bottom.

On the return loop you'll wander north through a peaceful residential neighborhood, viewing wonderful works of architecture up close. These include the massive Beaux-Arts Queen Anne High School (now condos) and an eye-popping Victorian cottage with a national reputation.

Your initial descent back down the hillside follows a moderately steep trail angling down toward the Aurora underpass at Dexter Way. We also offer directions for a shorter "lollipop loop" back down the Galer stairways. If you stay on the main route, the Dexter Way underpass is an attraction in itself, covered by a simple, vivid mural of the Puget Sound landscape. A final 82-step stairway lands you back at the marina.

Length:	**3.7 miles (3 miles with the optional Short Return via the Galer Stairs)**
Walking Time:	2 hours (short option 1 hour 30 minutes)
Steps Down:	300 (short option 621)
Steps Up:	476
Kid-Friendly:	This walk's "up" stairs are front-loaded, and the route is longish. A better bet is walk 11, "Southwest Queen Anne."
Cafes/Pubs:	You'll find lots of places near the turnaround point of your loop, around the Queen Anne Avenue–Galer Street junction.

Getting There: If you're driving, park in the lot at South Lake Union off Westlake Avenue N. The best entrance is marked by a stoplight where 8th Avenue N comes down from the north to merge with Westlake. The Westlake pedestrian overpass is just south of that stoplight, and we suggest you park south of the overpass. Parking time limits vary depending on where you park, so keep abreast of the signs. Mentro Transit Route 30 runs from Sand Point to the University District, via Ravenna.

From Lake Union up the Galer Stairs (284 steps up, 3 steps down): From the parking area, take the stairs up to the Westlake pedestrian overpass (1). This broad, strikingly designed suspension bridge makes you feel far away from the busy road beneath your feet. There are great views back toward Lake Union as well as up the hill in the direction you're headed. **WWW**

After the overpass, you switchback up three flights of stairs next to a commercial building. **WWW** Each successive level opens onto its own verdant plaza, with additional views of Lake Union, Downtown, and Capitol Hill. Look ahead to spot the antenna towers sitting at the top of Queen Anne Hill.

These switchbacking stairs lead to a crosswalk at Dexter Avenue N; a short stretch of Galer Street appears on the other side. Cross Dexter cautiously, then

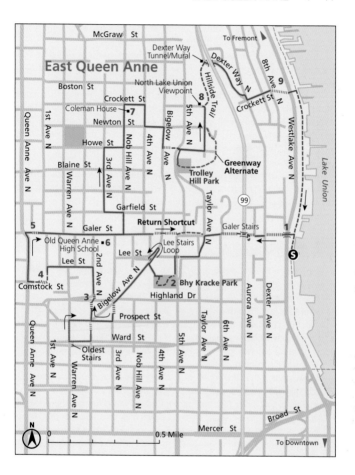

walk straight up the sidewalk to the Galer street-end. On the right, you'll find another stairway leading up to the Aurora Avenue N pedestrian overpass. The overpass, completed in 2005, is the only legal way pedestrians can cross Aurora anywhere along the eastern slope of Queen Anne.

There's a landing on the near side of Aurora Avenue, where your stairway meets up with the separate overpass stairway. As you start up, look for the automated wheelchair platform on one side of the overpass stairway (it requires a keycode to use), and the "runnel" on the other side, a tire-width ledge where bicyclists can push their bikes up the steps.

At the far side of the overpass, you step down three stairs to a landing. Turn right to start up the next section of the Galer stairs, 93 steps. From this point you'll be exploring the residential part of Queen Anne.

To Bhy Kracke Park (13 steps up): At the top of this flight of stairs, Galer Street briefly reappears. Head up Galer for one block, where it ends at Taylor Avenue N. Take the crosswalk across Taylor toward the base of yet another flight of Galer stairs, but instead of taking them, turn left onto the narrow sidewalk along Taylor. You're done with the Galer stairs for now, though they do continue up the hill ahead.

Taylor curves right, and soon you'll see another street merging from behind your right shoulder; this, too, is known as Taylor Avenue N, and it descends from the top of those stairs you passed a moment ago. Turn right at the next block, onto Lee Street.

BHY KRACKE, WHAT A VIEW!

Bhy Kracke Park is really three parks in one. The bottom level has a nice child's play area and a wisteria-draped pergola where weddings are sometimes held. A heavily vegetated hillside rises up behind, and in front there's a broad grassy area that comes forward to the street. It looks like a pleasant, traditional park space until you venture over to one of the barely visible walkways flanking the north and south sides. At this point you've entered "park number two," as the narrow walkway quickly takes you behind the first level, winding up the side of the hill and out of view behind the rhododendrons, vine maples, hazelnuts, magnolias, and other native and invasive plants competing for scarce space. About midway up you'll see a couple of semi-open side galleries where folks like to hang out, walk dogs, or catch some rays on a summer day. The "third park" is at the very top, where the pathway levels onto an open and neatly hardscaped plaza viewpoint (with drinking fountain). It offers probably the finest public panorama of Lake Union and Capitol Hill, the Space Needle, and Downtown. Bring your camera!

Bhy Kracke Park is named for the man who donated the land, Werner H. Kracke. As a play on his own name, he liked the old-fashioned exclamation "By cracky!" He came to Seattle in 1930 and lived at the top of this ravine until he retired to Hawaii in the 1960s. Eventually, he decided to donate the land to Seattle Parks, plus $20,000 toward its development. Kracke wanted this park to be a mini Butchart Gardens, and many of his ideas were used in the park's design.

A RING AROUND QUEEN ANNE

You may feel like there's something visually special about Bigelow Avenue. It is part of a network of variously named streets that almost completely encircle the hill, collectively known as "Queen Anne Boulevard." This whole network is listed on the Seattle Parks website as a 31-acre park.

In 1906 the citizens of Queen Anne petitioned the parks board to create a scenic boulevard around the hill. In part, their motivation was to make it easier to get around on Queen Anne Hill, which still had poor access in many areas. This proposal wasn't in the 1903 Olmsted plan, so the parks board was not favorable. In addition, the proposed route used normal street right-of-ways, providing much less than the 150-foot standard boulevard width needed for parklike landscaping.

Still, the citizens group prevailed after agreeing to partially pay for improvements, and Queen Anne Boulevard was incorporated into Seattle's boulevard plan. The route was finished in 1916, and today it's heavily used by neighborhood joggers and walkers. The roadway itself is under the jurisdiction of the City Engineer, but the landscaping remains part of the parks department. Its website says the boulevard offers "many possibilities for urban exploration: numerous alleyways, little side streets, 'hidden' stairways, and dead-end streets with views." You'll encounter Queen Anne Boulevard on the other two Queen Anne stairway walks as well.

Walk up Lee for a block until it ends in a 90-degree turn to the left, onto 5th Avenue N. Just after the turn, take the short flight of 13 steps from 5th Avenue up to—you guessed it—5th Avenue. At the top, turn left to follow 5th Avenue past two houses and then an apartment building on your right. Just past the building, turn right onto a sidewalk that curves left between the apartment building and a child's play area set back into a park. You're now in the lower section of Bhy Kracke Park (2).

The path curves up behind the play area and makes a couple of hairpin turns as it weaves up the hillside. From the top you can enjoy the wonderful view and use the drinking fountain. **WWW** There are several enviable homes with great views just a few feet north of the park, across Comstock Place. When you're ready, head out of the northwest side of the park and up a short stretch of Comstock Place that climbs to Bigelow Avenue N.

From Bhy Kracke Park to the Hidden Comstock Stairs (111 steps up, 155 steps down): At this point the route makes a mini-loop. As you approach

"Grand Dame" of Seattle stairways, the Comstock stairs

Bigelow after exiting Bhy Kracke Park, you'll notice there's no sidewalk on the near side, so cross Bigelow to the gravel path on the other side. Then turn right (heading northeast), passing a stairway coming down from the left and then a classic 1920s-era retaining wall. Behind that wall is Lee Street, angling down to meet you ahead.

When you reach Lee, make a hairpin turn left, to head southwest. When Lee curves away to the right, you'll see a short set of stairs to the left. Head down these stairs to complete your mini-loop.

At the bottom of the stairs turn right, back onto Bigelow. The Comstock Place exit you'll take from Bhy Kracke Park is just across the street, and ahead of you stretches a tree-lined boulevard of beautiful homes.

In one block you'll come to an angled intersection with Highland Drive. Keep straight on Bigelow, but get over to its left side. As you cross Highland, 3rd Avenue N also drops in from the right, transforming into a short set of stairs on the left side of Bigelow.

Just a few steps beyond the intersection, turn left down the 3rd Avenue stairs. There is very attractive landscaping at the top, and to the left is a modern home with arched roof and cedar sides—and an exceptional view to the south. At the bottom of the stairs, continue a few feet down 3rd Avenue, then turn right onto Prospect Street. At the next intersection with 2nd Avenue, you'll have a decision to make (see "Option: Side Trip to Seattle's Oldest Stairs"). If you choose to continue on the main route, turn right again onto 2nd Avenue, going north and up toward your next stairs.

Option: Side Trip to Seattle's Oldest Stairs (75 steps down)

The Seattle Department of Transportation keeps a list of stairways in Seattle, with all kinds of data, including age. The oldest listed stairway in Seattle was built in 1904, only two blocks from here.

For a quick trip to see it, turn south on 2nd, and head down 75 steps to the street below. A few yards later, when you arrive at Ward Street, turn right. At the next block—the intersection of Ward and Warren Avenue N—you'll be at the top of Seattle's oldest stairs (42 steps). To complete the loop, walk north on Warren to Prospect, then turn right. Then walk one more block back to your starting place at 2nd Avenue N. ♦

As you walk north on 2nd Avenue from Prospect Street, you'll quickly come to the first of several stairs on Queen Anne that feature a classic early-1900s design: generously broad steps and low-slung, thick concrete sides with deeply inset decorative patterns and a substantial rounded cap (3). In summer this stairway's entrance is deeply shrouded by trees, which adds a sense of mystery to its appeal.

At the top of these stairs you'll emerge briefly onto Highland Drive; angle across and to the right, and take the next set of stairs up to meet 2nd Avenue N as it continues north. Keep going up 2nd for one block, then turn left onto cobblestoned Lee Street.

After a block, at Warren Avenue N, the cobblestone surface returns to asphalt. You'll see a water tower emerge on the right, next to the firehouse. It's built near Queen Anne Hill's highest point, 456 feet.

At the next junction, turn left onto 1st Avenue N. Here 1st Avenue is just a lane heading south between houses, with a narrow sidewalk along the left.

THE COUNTERBALANCE

Between 1901 and 1940, a web of electric railcar lines served various parts of Queen Anne Hill. On Queen Anne Avenue, the grade between Mercer and Comstock is so steep—up to 18.5 percent—that extra power was needed to help the railcars get safely up and down the hill. That extra power was supplied by gravity.

In a tunnel beneath the passenger car tracks, two squat 16-ton unpowered railcars ran up and down the hill. Each of these counterbalance cars was permanently connected to a cable that ran through a pulley at the top of the grade. The free end of each car's cable could be attached to a passenger railcar as needed. A passenger car at the bottom of the hill, for instance, would be connected to the counterbalance car at the top end. The heavy counterbalance car would then be released downhill, pulling the passenger car up toward the pulley as it went. Conversely, a car heading down the steep hill would be held back as it lugged the counterbalance car up from the bottom. Through 1940, this system enabled passenger railcars to maintain a safe and steady 8-miles-per-hour speed up and down Queen Anne Hill.

Where the lane ends, take the sidewalk on ahead. Where the sidewalk ends, turn right. You've just discovered the gorgeous Comstock stairs (4)!

The luxuriant greenery along the way, and the ivy draping itself over the sides of the stairway, makes these stairs look especially spectacular at the height of summer. These elegantly curving steps, built in 1909, exhibit all the hallmarks of the golden era of stair construction in Seattle. They qualify as "hidden" because you can't see them from any street at the top, and the bottom is so far back from Queen Anne Avenue N that it's practically invisible to passing traffic.

The Galer–Queen Anne Stairs (68 steps up): After exiting the Comstock stairs, head down the narrow cobblestone lane, W Comstock Street. A few dozen yards down, Comstock runs into Queen Anne Avenue, where you'll turn right.

Queen Anne Avenue was originally named "Temperance Avenue" by David Denny, one of the original settlers of Lower Queen Anne (and younger brother of Arthur, who led the Denny Party to Alki in 1851). David was considered politically progressive, which at the time meant being for women's right to vote and against discriminatory laws aimed at Chinese immigrants. It also meant opposing the sale of alcohol. "Temperance Avenue" didn't stick around long, though: an 1899 map of Seattle already uses the name "Queen Anne Avenue."

The famous Queen Anne Counterbalance ran up Queen Anne Avenue just as far as where you stand. Counterbalance Park honors that history, just a few blocks down the hill at Roy Street.

After turning right onto Queen Anne Avenue, walk up the hill two blocks to Galer Street, where Queen Anne Avenue makes a little jog to the left. As you walk toward the first crosswalk at the Galer intersection, you'll see another elegant stairway heading up from your right (5). This is a good junction for a break, with several cafes and restaurants nearby. When you're ready, take the Galer–Queen Anne stairs on up. These beautiful stairs are extra-wide, with a handrail down the middle. When you reach the top, continue east for three blocks.

To Old Queen Anne High School: From the top of the Galer–Queen Anne stairs, you'll pass four streets on the right to arrive at the old Queen Anne High School (6), built in 1909. This large, magnificent Beaux-Arts building is a Seattle Landmark and on the National Register of Historic Places. WWW The high school was closed in 1981 and turned into apartments, then converted to condos in 2006.

Here's where you decide whether to continue with the main route or take a shortened return via the Galer stairs (see "Option: Short Return via the Galer Stairs"). The main route has one section that follows a narrow and moderately steep trail down the side of Queen Anne Hill. Walkers used to mountain trails will be just fine under dry conditions, but we recommend the short option for everybody in wet weather. The short option is also a lovely, scenic alternative if you don't feel like navigating the hillside trail on the main route.

The main route continues north past an amazing polychrome Queen Anne Victorian cottage and on to an out-of-the-way viewpoint, with great views of north Lake Union and Gas Works Park. Then it angles down the forested hillside on the aforementioned trail, to the mural-covered Dexter Way tunnel beneath Aurora Avenue. Finally, you'll walk down the 82 steps of the Crockett stairs toward Westlake Marina and the end of your loop.

Option: Short Return via the Galer Stairs (501 steps down, 3 up)

From Queen Anne High School (6) you can shave 0.7 mile from the main route by doubling back down the Galer stair complex. Aside from shortening the walk, you also get a 180-degree change in perspective, with many wonderful views of Lake Union and the city. You'll also step down a very nice section of the Galer stairs that you missed coming up.

From Queen Anne High School, continue east on Galer until you reach 4th Avenue N at a Y intersection, with Galer veering left and 4th turning at a sharper angle to the right. You'll see your next stairs just off the 4th Avenue side of the Y.

These stairs switch to pathway and then back to stairs before opening onto a crosswalk at Bigelow Avenue N. Cross Bigelow and start down your next, longer flight of stairs, which end at yet another brief section of Galer

Street. Continue down Galer to another short set of stairs, the street itself veering off to the right as Taylor Avenue N. After this short flight you'll be heading down the same section of the Galer complex you climbed earlier. Just keep going down the Galer right-of way, enjoying the reverse views. Your stairway walk ends at the base of the stairs dropping down to the marina parking lot from the Westlake pedestrian overpass. ♦

From Queen Anne High School to a Spectacular Victorian Cottage: To continue on the main route, walk east past old Queen Anne High School, and turn left onto Nob Hill Avenue N. In one block turn left again onto Garfield Street, going west. After a block you'll have circled around to the front entrance of John Hay Elementary, opposite 3rd Avenue N. The entryway to the school has some interesting artwork, including colorful sidewalk mosaics. **WWW**

Turn up 3rd Avenue N, walking through three blocks of quiet residential streets. When you reach Howe, turn right, then one block later make a left onto Nob Hill Avenue. After you pass through the next intersection at Newton Street, start looking for an amazing Victorian-style cottage several houses up on the right (7). **WWW**

Brian Coleman has spent more than twenty years transforming this 1906 Craftsman cottage into a lavish and colorful Victorian confection. Among the many surprising details: a flower box at the right front window with a hand-carved sculpture of alligators harassing an anxious-looking infant, and the Latin motto carved around the middle of the elaborate turret, which translates to "The more the better." For more details about this cool house, go to www.oldhousejournal.com and search for "Brian Coleman."

To North Lake Union Viewpoint via Trolley Hill Park (60 steps down): From the Coleman house, continue a few feet north to Crockett Street and turn right. Go one block east on Crockett to 4th Avenue N and turn right again. You'll be walking south on 4th Avenue N, with historic, turreted "Old" John Hay School (1905) behind the chainlink fence to the left. **WWW** This fine wood-frame structure has two octagonal turrets framing the entrance; inside there are wide wooden hallways, lined on either side by cream-colored arches that are supported by delicate columns of beautifully worked dark wood. Today "Old" John Hay School is a Seattle Landmark.

At the next corner, turn left onto Newton Street, then right at the next block onto Bigelow Avenue N—the same road you walked after leaving Bhy Kracke Park, though now you're several blocks north. In one block you'll reach Howe Street, with the top of a stairway just visible on your left. Take the 60 steps down to a lane next to an apartment building, staying straight ahead until you emerge at 5th Avenue N.

Turn right at 5th Avenue N and head south until you approach the end of the sidewalk. Here you'll see the Trolley Hill Park entrance across the street. It's flanked by two stone-block plinths that are topped by decorative wooden sculptures. WWW Once you're safely across this busy arterial, it's time to check out the park!

Trolley Hill Park is named after the trolley line that used to run along 5th Avenue N. With views and a neighborhood P-Patch garden, it's a place well worth exploring, especially the southeast end of the park where timber steps lead down to a trail that arcs north through a sloping greenbelt toward MacLean Park and Newton Street. (You can take this trail, marked "Greenway Alternate" on the map as an alternate route, meeting up with the main route where Newton climbs up from the greenbelt to meet Taylor Avenue.)

To resume, turn right onto the sidewalk from the park entrance, curving north up 5th Avenue. Take a right onto Howe Street, then a left at the next block onto Taylor Avenue N. As you walk up the right-hand sidewalk, you'll see MacLean Park's strategically placed benches looking out toward Lake Union.

Keep walking north on Taylor Avenue, past Newton Street, until it ends at Crockett Street. Here, tucked into the elbow of Taylor and Crockett, you'll find a waist-high, moss-topped concrete wall (8), built in the style of those older staircases you saw earlier. Standing at the wall, you get a great angle across north Lake Union toward Gas Works Park and the I-5 Bridge. There's even a glimpse of Lake Washington on the other side of Capitol Hill. WWW

North Lake Union Viewpoint to the Crockett Stairs and End (82 steps down): At the south end of the wall (8), take a few stairsteps to the path that angles down the hillside from here to Aurora Avenue. You'll be doing a bit of trail hiking along this stretch, which isn't especially scenic until you get to the Dexter Way murals at the bottom. There are lots of maple trees and generous amounts of ivy covering the ground on either side of the path. On your right, the hillside drops toward Aurora Avenue.

At the bottom of the path, turn right alongside Dexter Way, which at this point is just an off-ramp from southbound Aurora. It almost immediately ducks under Aurora via a tunnel that's covered with cool mural art, inside and out. WWW The design, inspired by Mount Rainier's landscape, was painted by volunteers. A neighborhood sponsor group teamed up with Urban ArtWorks on this project, one of 400 murals scattered all over the city.

Once you're through the tunnel underpass, continue on Dexter Way as it angles down to meet Dexter Avenue N. Take the crosswalk to the far side of the avenue and turn right onto the sidewalk. There's a small grocery just before you reach Crockett Street, where you'll turn left. Walk down the hill on Crockett a couple of blocks until it ends in a set of stairs, at 8th Avenue N (9).

At the bottom of the Crockett stairs, take the nearby signaled crosswalk across Westlake Avenue N. WWW Continue straight into the marina parking lot until you reach the pedestrian walkway near the water. Turn right, and stroll a pleasant 0.4 mile back to the Westlake pedestrian overpass and the end of your walk.

11   Southwest Queen Anne

Up the Lower Galer Stairs from 9th Avenue W

The three stairway walks on Queen Anne Hill are like siblings: recognizably related, but with notably different personalities. Southwest Queen Anne is the elegant, stately one. Its sedate streets and cobblestone lanes are lined with immense trees and historic landmark homes on large lots. Its public infrastructure is beautiful and grandly scaled, with a generous sprinkling of pocket parks and expansive views.

This part of Queen Anne was settled by some of Seattle's most successful entrepreneurs and civic leaders. They leveraged their clout with the City, and their wealth, to construct Queen Anne Boulevard around the hill—in spite of the fact it wasn't in the city's original boulevard plan. Not only that, the crowning part of the boulevard—the elaborate West Queen Anne (or Wilcox) Wall—is located here.

The historic homes in the Southwest Queen Anne neighborhood were built during a uniquely prosperous time. Except for several years lost to the Panic of 1893, the decades that straddled the two centuries were a time of soaring economic activity. Fortunes were made in a fast-growing Seattle; Downtown was rebuilt and expanded after the devastating 1889 fire, and the Klondike gold rush of the late 1890s was supplied from Seattle. Lucrative new service businesses were constructed around a booming core of extractive industries, banking, and real-estate development. This was the time when opulent homes and beautiful infrastructure *could* be built, and view-rich Southwest Queen Anne was just the place to do it.

Length:	**2.6 miles**
Walking Time:	1 hour 20 minutes
Steps Down:	588
Steps Up:	477
Kid-Friendly:	The entire walk is doable for kids above age seven. Younger kids might enjoy a walk that centers around Lower Kerry Park, which has a play area with an amazing slide. **WWW** Parking is available along Highland Drive at the top of the park, but restrooms are harder to come by; they can be found in the coffee shops/cafes along Galer Street between 3rd and 4th avenues, four blocks north. From Kerry Park it's an easy walk west along Highland to main attractions like Parsons Gardens, Marshall Park, and the Wilcox Wall. You can try this fun little two-stairway circuit: from Highland, walk north up 6th, left onto W Comstock, and left again onto Willard Avenue W, passing Parsons Gardens on the way back down to Highland.
Cafes/Pubs:	There are several cafes on Galer Street between 3rd and 4th, near the loop's start/end. An impromptu picnic at one of the view parks along Highland Drive (Kerry, Parsons Gardens, Marshall) can be provisioned by the Trader Joe's, at Galer and 1st Avenue W.

Southwest Queen Anne

N

0.3 Mile

Galer St

Lee St

Highland Dr

Queen Anne

Ballard-Howe Residence

Ave N

1st Ave W

2nd Ave W

W Garfield St

W Galer St

W Comstock St

3rd Ave W

Stimson-Griffiths Residence

W Highland Dr

7

Kerry Park

Play Area

3rd Ave W

4th Ave W

W Lee St

6

W Prospect St

W Kinnear Pl

W Garfield St

W Galer St

5th Ave W

McFee/Klockzien Residence

West Queen Anne School

8

S

6th Ave W

Charles H. Black Residence

Parsons Residence

W Olympic Pl

W Blaine St

6th Ave W

Willard Ave W

Parsons Gardens

W Garfield St

7th Ave W

Waechter House

Betty Bowen Viewpoint

Marshall Park

W Mercer Pl

1

8th Ave W

3

Wall

5

8th Ave W

Wilcox

Wall

Wilcox

W Lee St

4

Way W

9th Ave W

2

W Galer St

Olympic

Elliott Ave W

To Downtown ▶

To Ballard ▶

Getting There: Metro Transit Route 2 stops at the beginning of the route, at Galer and either 5th or 6th, depending on your direction. MT2 runs between Madrona and West Queen Anne via First Hill, Downtown, and Seattle Center. If you're driving, head west on Galer Street from its junction with Queen Anne Avenue, and park along Galer between 4th and 6th. Space here is unrestricted and usually plentiful.

To the Upper Garfield Stairs and Wilcox Wall (98 steps down): From your starting place near Galer and 6th Avenue W, turn north up 6th. After one block turn left onto Garfield Street and walk west for two and a half blocks to the top of the upper Garfield stairs. `WWW`

At the bottom of the stairs you'll reach the upper half of 8th Avenue W. Directly across, seemingly blocking further progress, stretches the famous Wilcox Wall (1). `WWW`

Here, the main route descends the wall via a grand stairway to the lower half of 8th, before moving ahead to the lower Garfield stairs. To get there, just step across the street toward the elaborate twin lamp posts, where you'll find two opposing stairways leading down. To the south, about 0.3 mile from here, you'll encounter another section of the wall with even grander dual stairways.

FAMOUS AND FABULOUS WILCOX WALL

A long line of colorful retaining walls and stairs runs along the western side of this stairway route, looking like some combination of Art Deco and Gothic. They feature elaborate cast-iron light fixtures, decorative brickwork in vivid red diamond-lattice patterns, and flying buttresses to support the street above. On close inspection you'll even see the grain patterns pressed into the concrete by the wooden forms used during pouring.

The Wilcox Wall, or more officially the "West Queen Anne Walls," runs 0.4 mile north–south along 8th Avenue W and 8th Place W. Over most of that distance the wall sections separate the high and low lanes of 8th Avenue W, varying in height from 4 to 22 feet. Locals love to stroll along the top, taking in Puget Sound on one side and the large, lovely homes on the other. The wall was designed by Walter Wilcox and built in 1913 as part of Queen Anne Boulevard, a system of linked streets encircling Queen Anne Hill (for more about Queen Anne Boulevard, see the previous walk, 10, "East Queen Anne"). This beautiful type of construction can also be found along 7th Avenue W, between Howe and Crockett streets. The wall was designated a Seattle Landmark in 1976.

The wall also continues north from here, for about 0.1 mile. You can explore this short stretch of the wall on a quick side trip (see "Option: Exploring Wilcox Wall").

Option: Exploring Wilcox Wall

To explore more of the Wilcox Wall to the north, after crossing 8th Avenue N (1) turn right on the sidewalk next to the wall, rather than taking the stairs down. As you go, the street curves 90 degrees right to become W Blaine Street, just before it reaches 7th Avenue N. At 7th Avenue, hook back around in the opposite direction to get onto the lower half of Blaine, which is a narrow cobblestone lane. At the next intersection turn left onto the lower half of 8th Avenue and walk south, back to Garfield, with the wall at your left side. This detour takes you the long way around to the bottom side of the Wilcox Wall, adding almost 0.3 mile along with extensive views of the wall from above and below. ◆

Lower Garfield Stairs and the Galer Stairs (66 steps down, 169 steps up): Once you've made your way to the lower side of the Wilcox Wall (1) **WWW**, continue west on Garfield for a little more than one block. At the next street-end you'll see the top of the lower Garfield stairs. In winter especially, this spot offers nice views of the Magnolia Bridge and Interbay, as well as Smith Cove, Elliott Bay Marina, and Bainbridge Island. At the bottom of these stairs, turn left onto the sidewalk running along the uphill half of 9th Avenue W (on the opposite side you can see a narrow walkway angling down to the lower half of the street).

Continue your exploration by walking south on the uphill side of 9th Avenue, until you reach W Galer Street. Here on the left you'll see the base of the lower Galer stairs heading up from the sidewalk (2). During summer, a low-hanging maple tree may obscure these stairs until you're on top of them. In fall, the bright yellow leaves make an eye-catching contrast to the English ivy groundcover and the stairs themselves. The first flight of 34 stairs is followed by a short walkway, with graceful private stairs and paths along both flanks. A second flight of 57 stairs ends in a short stretch of cobblestoned street heading toward 8th Avenue W.

Cross 8th Avenue, plunging straight up a short walkway just to the left of an elaborately balconied-and-balustraded home. **WWW** On the right, just before the upper Galer stairs begin, a massive European beech towers above. Large conifers line the upper reaches of the stairway, giving it a distinctive woodsy feel. The stairs are briefly interrupted by a small lane, then come to an end with a short stretch of walkway that meets 7th Avenue W.

The Lee Stairs via the Wilcox Wall (227 steps down): Cross 7th Avenue, walking ahead a short block to Willard Avenue W. Turn right onto Willard and walk south one block. Just before turning right onto W Lee Street, take a look kitty-corner to the left.

Largely hidden behind a wall of trees and shrubs is a huge Tudor Revival house that's a Seattle Landmark. The view from any angle never gets much better than this, as the house sits at the center of a tree-ringed "country" estate that occupies the entire block. It's the Charles H. Black House, completed in 1909. Mr. Black founded the Seattle Hardware Company in 1883, building his fortune a dozen years later by supplying miners during the Klondike gold rush. We'll point out this mysterious property a couple of times again, from different angles. The landscaping was designed by Olmsted Brothers, the famous firm that designed Seattle's scenic park-and-boulevard system, beginning in 1903.

At this point W Lee Street is essentially a driveway heading west, ending quickly in a little cul-de-sac. There you'll find the upper Lee stairs, which were built in 1908 but sport newly installed double handrails. **WWW** To the right of the stairs, a massive timber retaining wall accompanies you to the bottom.

At the base of the stairs turn left onto 7th Avenue W, then turn right at the next opportunity, back onto a neatly cobblestoned section of W Lee Street.

Just after you turn right, at 700 W Lee, there's a residential stairway entrance with subtle tile decorations on either side. These private stairs wind up through gardens to a multi-gabled Tudor Revival house and Seattle Landmark, the Waechter House (1915). The house has exotic associations: the original owner, Ollie Waechter, headed up a company called Siberian Fish and Storage, which ran the Soviet government's cured-salmon packing concession at the mouth of

GRAND STAIRWAY ON THE WILCOX WALL

From atop the Wilcox Wall near W Lee Street there are spectacular views of Magnolia and Puget Sound and, weather permitting, the Olympic Mountains. Just in front of the marina and shipping terminal, you can see the Amgen manufacturing complex and a sliver of the Amgen helix bridge and stairs, partly hidden by foreground buildings on the left.

Built into this part of the wall is one of the must-see Seattle stairways (3). Reminiscent of the colorful Art Deco/Gothic Garfield stairs you saw earlier, these stairs are considerably taller and more complex in design. Like the Garfield stairs, this set has two descending flights, but in this case the upper entrances are separated by about 80 feet. As they head downward, the two flights converge at a wide landing about a third of the way down. From there they separate again, bottoming out at the same distance from each other as they are at the top. It's difficult to take in the complex layout of these stairs, honeycombed as they are with floors, ceilings, arches, and flying buttresses!

Famous and fabulous Wilcox Wall

the Kamchatka River into the early 1930s. In 1938, the house was rented by the general manager of the Japanese shipping line NYK. It's said that the Sound view made it an ideal place for the Japanese to gather intelligence during the period of increasing international tensions just before World War II.

At the bottom of W Lee, cross the now-familiar upper 8th Avenue W, over to the sidewalk that runs atop a grand section of the Wilcox Wall (3). **WWW** The lower half of 8th Avenue lies below.

To find the top of the grand Wilcox Wall stairway, walk south a few yards on the sidewalk after you've crossed 8th Avenue from Lee Street. The 72 stairs of the northern flight will carry you down to the lower half of 8th Avenue at the base of the wall. Turn right onto the lower half of 8th Avenue. Later, you'll loop back to the base, near the bottom of the southern flight.

In a few steps you'll see the top of the lower Lee stairs on your left, marked by a street sign. After the first 55 stairs you'll cross a lane and then follow a short walkway before stepping down a final few stairs, to 9th Avenue W.

Highland Stairs and the Hidden Wilcox Trail (62 steps up): From W Lee Street, turn left onto 9th Avenue and stay on the east sidewalk as 9th Avenue merges with Olympic Way. The Highland stairs come up quickly on the left, but a retaining wall and foliage will likely obscure them right up to the last moment.

Head up the Highland stairs (4), with views of the Wilcox Wall above. The stairs end at the lower half of 8th Avenue W. From there, take the narrow concrete walkway that starts just a few feet to your left, angling toward the upper half of 8th.

At the top of the walkway, turn left onto upper 8th Avenue W, then walk past the two homes on your right. Just before you reach the base of the southern flight of the Wilcox Wall stairs, take the "hidden trail" off to the right. It runs between the base of the wall and the backyards of those homes you just passed. Queen Anne Boulevard/8th Place W runs overhead; you can see the sidewalk portion jutting out of the wall. Rest assured, this somewhat obscure trail runs along the Queen Anne Boulevard right-of-way. (WWW)

Marshall Park and Parsons Gardens (57 steps up): After the short stretch of "hidden trail" along the base of the gracefully curving Wilcox Wall, you'll encounter a third set of stairs, complete with the trademark cast-iron light pole at the base. When you reach the top of the wall, you'll be right next to Marshall Park/Betty Bowen Viewpoint (5; see "She Shaped Today's Seattle"). With the right weather, views of Puget Sound and the Olympics can be stunning.

SHE SHAPED TODAY'S SEATTLE

Betty Bowen was an assistant director at the Seattle Art Museum who also supported a broad range of civic and environmental causes around the city. Her legacy continues to be felt in Seattle and beyond: alongside architect Victor Steinbrueck, she worked to save Pike Place Market in the 1970s, and she befriended and helped young artists and writers like Morris Graves and Tom Robbins. Betty Bowen Viewpoint (5), designed by Steinbrueck, is essentially a couple of seating areas set into Marshall Park. Reflecting her strong connection to the arts, eleven prominent artists memorialized Bowen by contributing works to the site, including nine sketches transferred to concrete along the edge of the upper seating area. A nearby plaque identifies the artists and the locations of their works.

Your next stop is Parsons Gardens just north across the street from Betty Bowen Viewpoint. There's a small side entrance along W Highland Drive, but the main entrance gate is clearly visible kitty-corner from Marshall Park, across 7th Avenue W.

Once inside, you can follow a secretive gravel path around the circumference, and exit where you entered. This lovely garden has a central grassy area surrounded by flowering shrubs and ornamental trees. WWW In the sunny summer months you might find people sunning on beach towels, reading or dozing in this quiet clearing. The garden used to be part of the residential grounds of the Parsons Residence next door, but in 1956 the family donated it to the city (more about the Parsons Residence when you walk past it later). Today, the garden is sometimes used for small parties or wedding ceremonies.

Exit Parsons Gardens out of either gate and walk uphill on 7th Avenue W.

Parsons Gardens to Lower Kerry Park (45 steps up, 145 steps down): After one block on 7th, turn right and head uphill on W Comstock Street. It's another of the charming, narrow cobblestone streets in this area. WWW At the crest you'll see the top of a stairway on the right, behind a concrete traffic barrier. Kitty-corner to the left you can see the southwest corner of the block-filling Charles H. Black property; again, there isn't much to see, except a wall of trees.

Head down the 74 stairs to the street-end below, Willard Avenue W. As you walk down Willard, you'll pass between Parsons Gardens on the right and the Parsons Residence on the left. This Dutch Colonial house, built in 1905, is a Seattle Landmark. It's an impressive house, with a fireplace in every bedroom, a gym, a library, a conservatory, and a large sunroom.

Turn left onto W Highland Drive, where you'll get a front view of the Parsons Residence. At the next block turn left, up 6th Avenue W. To the right, as you walk toward your next stairs, you'll see the Tudor Revival McFee/Klockzien Residence (1909), another Seattle Landmark. WWW

HOW OLD ARE THESE STAIRS?

SDOT's database shows the stairway behind the McFee/Klockzien Residence was built a year before the house, in 1908. So far, the nod for oldest stairway in Seattle goes to one built in 1904 at Warren Avenue N between upper and lower Ward Streets, in Southeast Queen Anne. Several stairways you tread on this walk are almost as old; they include the lower Lee stairs and the Highland stairs (1907), and both the upper and lower Garfield stairs (1906). In fact, there's considerable missing age data in the SDOT stairway files, partly because many stairways in the city were built by other jurisdictions or by private parties. Where age data are missing, SDOT researches it case by case, as individual stairways come up for refurbishing or repair.

At the top of the 6th Avenue stairs you'll get another view of the Charles H. Black property, this time the southeast corner. According to www.HistoryLink .org, a tunnel connected the main house to stables that were located somewhere along the property's 6th Avenue border. Unfortunately, the house itself remains cloaked by tree cover from this angle as well.

Head east on W Comstock, then after one block turn right onto 5th Avenue W. After another block, turn left onto W Highland Drive. The next landmark is at 405 W Highland, on the south side of the street: the Stimson-Griffiths Residence (6), listed on the National Register of Historic Places. The house is partly veiled by mature landscaping and trees. As you pass, look for the vivid patterned panel running across the width of the large third-floor gable. The house, built in 1905, combines two styles: Swiss Chalet (broad gables, decorative trussing, articulated corner balconies) and Tudor Revival (half-timber construction, irregularity of overall plan). The original owner, Fred Stimson, operated a large lumber mill in Ballard. His family moved out of this house in 1910, to a country property in Woodinville—today's Chateau Ste. Michelle winery.

Just beyond the Stimson-Griffiths Residence, look for a concrete traffic barrier on the right, at 4th Avenue W. It marks a sidewalk that runs a fair distance in from the street before reaching the top of your next stairway, with 71 steps.

Not far down the stairs, on the right, look for where the handrail bends around the trunk of a massive tree. **WWW** You can still see weld marks where the railing has been adjusted to accommodate the expanding tree.

At the bottom of the stairs, turn left onto W Prospect Street. Walk along the north side of the street for one block to your next set of stairs and the Lower Kerry Park play area. The play area is a neighborhood favorite, with all kinds of things to climb up, crawl over, swing on, and slide down.

Kerry Park's Classic Views (57 steps up): Take an intermittent series of 57 steps up the west side of Kerry Park to the upper level, with its famous views (7). Many Seattleites may not know exactly where Kerry Park is, but most of them have seen countless photos taken from this viewpoint. It's also very popular with out-of-town visitors and bus tours. There's no better place to take in the panorama from the Space Needle and Downtown, across Elliott Bay to Alki Point. Clouds permitting, Mount Rainier might put in a dazzling appearance.

Kerry Park began as a 1927 land gift from Seattle lumber baron Albert Kerry and his wife, Katherine, who wanted the city to use the land as a public viewpoint. Albert was a gifted civic organizer for Seattle around the turn of the twentieth century. Among many accomplishments, he played a leading role in organizing the 1909 Exposition and, as president of the Seattle Chamber of Commerce, he oversaw the construction of the grand Olympic Hotel downtown (now the Fairmont Olympic Hotel).

An Architectural Finale (52 steps down, 87 steps up): From the viewpoint, walk on W Highland Drive to the eastern side of Kerry Park. There, at 2nd Avenue W, you'll find a set of stairs dropping down to where 2nd Avenue picks up again, as a short stretch of cobblestone lane. Turn left onto W Prospect Street to begin the last leg of your loop.

The block here has beautiful residences on either side, with a couple of large apartment buildings looming behind the homes on the north side. At the next corner, as you turn left onto 1st Avenue W, you'll round an interesting low-slung Northwest Contemporary home, with huge windows in front and a variety of art pieces in the yard. You can see your next stairs zigzagging up the hill ahead. **WWW**

After one 90-degree turn and 87 steps, the 1st Avenue stairs deposit you back on W Highland Drive. Kitty-corner to the right sits the Neoclassical Revival Ballard-Howe Residence (1901). This stately home's architectural details include a massive entry portico supported by Ionian columns (echoed by pilasters at the corners of the house), and a second, circular front porch nested inside. This structure is a Seattle Landmark, and is listed on the National Register of Historic Places. The original house extends only to the windows on either side of the entry portico; the rest is a 1930s add-on, when the house was sold at a loss during the Depression and converted to apartments.

Just across 1st Avenue from the Ballard-Howe Residence are the beautiful Victoria Apartments (1921), now condos. They're laid out in a horseshoe shape, with a large central garden in the middle. The building is beautifully proportioned, with nice terra-cotta details standing out from the red brick walls. Before a large apartment building was constructed across the street, the Victoria Apartments must have enjoyed brilliant views of the city and Elliott Bay.

From Highland Drive, walk north up 1st Avenue W. Turn left at the next block, W Comstock Street, and then right two blocks later, onto 3rd Avenue W. Two blocks after that, turn left onto W Galer Street. From here, you can stop at one of several coffee shops or cafes on the way back to your starting point.

As you walk up Galer between 5th and 6th, note the massive dark-red brick building on the south side, with steeply sloped roof and arched windows (8). The "WEST QUEEN ANNE SCHOOL" sign under an arched entryway on Galer gives away the building's original identity. The school was opened in 1896, closed for good 85 years later, and converted to condos a few years after that. At the time, this condo conversion was the largest public-to-private repurposing project in the Northwest, and it became a national model for recycling historic public school buildings. Today, this grand old Romanesque pile is a Seattle Landmark, and on the National Register of Historic Places.

12 Northwest Queen Anne

The route's first stairs, at the end of 13th Avenue

One day, speeding north on 15th Avenue W toward Ballard, we happened to glimpse a stairway disappearing up the hill. On a curious impulse we turned off the road and went looking for it, and that began our fascination with these "scenic byways," the stairways of Seattle.

Those steps turned out to be the Wheeler stairs, which rise in multiple flights to Rachel's Playground, with its peaceful setting and fine views. From there we found ourselves wandering all over Northwest Queen Anne, exploring a neighborhood that was completely new to us.

This walk doesn't cover the entire length of the Wheeler stairs, but you will climb several of its flights up to Rachel's Playground. You'll see lots of this neighborhood's nooks and crannies and enjoy great western vistas toward Magnolia, Interbay, and even Alki Point.

Of the three Queen Anne stairway walks, this is the one with the low-key, unflashy personality. It's not rich in architectural treasures, and the industrial and commercial Interbay is just downslope to the west. But like its counterparts, Northwest Queen Anne has marvelous views and gorgeous steps, and an interesting ambience all its own.

Length:	**3 miles**
Walking Time:	1 hour 30 minutes
Steps Down:	308
Steps Up:	216
Kid-Friendly:	Kids will love Rachel's Playground, about 0.7 mile round-trip, and you'll like the view. **WWW** From the start at W Boston Street, head straight up the Boston stairs. At the top, take a few steps right up Gilman Drive W, then cross over to 12th Avenue W (carefully—Gilman is an arterial without a crosswalk). Turn back toward the left, walking north along 12th Avenue W. Follow the uphill lane of 12th Avenue, and then turn right onto Wheeler Street. Take the stairs ahead, right up into Rachel's Playground. There are no restroom facilities along the route.
Cafes/Pubs:	Peet's Coffee and Whole Foods are nearby on 15th Avenue W.

Getting There: If you're driving, park on W Boston Street anywhere on the block east of 14th Avenue W. Drivers going north- or southbound on 15th Avenue along Interbay can turn east onto Boston, just across the street from the building with the lime-green highlights (Seattle Animal Shelter). Drivers coming down Queen Anne Hill along Gilman can make a sharp left onto 14th, and again a block later, to get parked and positioned on Boston. If you're taking the bus, RapidRide D Line runs between Downtown, Ballard, and north to Crown Hill, with stops along 15th.

To Gilman Drive via the 13th Avenue Stairs (63 steps up, 20 steps down): At the corner of W Boston Street and 13th Avenue W, note the stairs straight ahead **WWW** but turn right, onto the downhill side of 13th (we'll save those stairs until the end of your loop). Continue along 13th just past Newton Street and up the tree-canopied stairs ahead (1). At the top, take the 90-degree left turn onto a lengthy walkway, it, too, running beneath the shelter of heavy tree canopy.

Toward the end of the walkway there's a discreet, two-tiered play area on your left. Closer inspection reveals steps leading down to a long steel slide built right into the slope. **WWW** The end of the walkway deposits you onto 12th Avenue W; turn left onto 12th, then take the short stairway on the right at the street-end. After those stairs the street resumes, and when it divides, bear right.

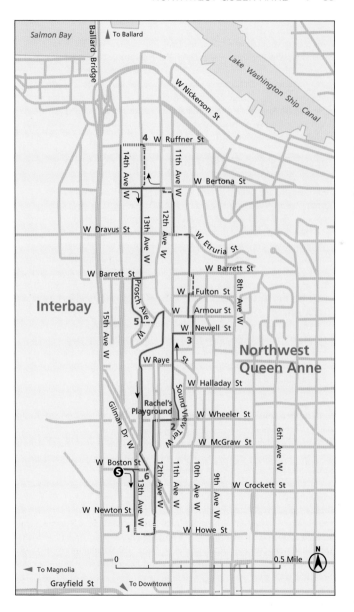

You'll soon arrive at Gilman Drive W, an arterial. There's a crosswalk a few yards over to your left; carefully cross over and continue up 12th Avenue.

To the Wheeler Stairs and Rachel's Playground (79 steps up): Past Gilman, 12th Avenue divides again. This time take the left side, past the "DO NOT ENTER" wrong-way traffic sign, following the sidewalk on the left. Soon, you'll spot a stairway on the right, climbing up the side of the wall separating the two halves of 12th Avenue. Head up the stairs, and at the top cross 12th and continue straight ahead on W Wheeler Street. You'll see more stairs straight ahead, leading up to Rachel's Playground (2).

RACHEL'S PLAYGROUND: A MEMORIAL

On January 31, 2000, Alaska Airlines Flight 261, en route to Seattle from Puerto Vallarta, crashed into the ocean off California, killing all aboard. Two nearby Queen Anne families were on the flight.

The official name of the small park and playground (2) straddling the Wheeler stairs is Soundview Terrace Park. One of the passengers on the flight, six-year-old Rachel Pearson, visited Soundview Terrace Park often to play. In honor of Rachel and the families, neighbors renovated the park and added the playground to its south section, naming it after Rachel. Volunteers continue to care for the park and its beautiful landscaping.

The north section of the park is a grassy terrace area with a couple of comfy game tables. There are also strategically placed benches around the park, perfect for taking in the views of Magnolia and beyond. A walkway connects the two sections, rambling north through the park until it reaches Sound View Terrace W.

To the Newell and Armour Stairs (57 steps up, 39 steps down): At the top of the stairs out of Rachel's Playground, turn left onto Sound View Terrace W. As you pass above the northern boundary of the park, note the small seating area next to a circular terrace of granite pavers. Bronze compass markers are set into the terrace, pointing out the directions of your favorite views.

For the next few minutes you'll be walking north through a quiet, scenic neighborhood of well-kept Craftsman-style homes. Sound View Terrace soon merges with 11th Avenue W, continuing north past W Raye and W Bothwell streets. When you reach W Newell Street, turn right. At the street-end, climb the 57 steps of the Newell stairs (3) **WWW** to 10th Avenue W, part of Queen Anne Boulevard (see walk 10, "East Queen Anne"). At the top of the stairs, take a minute to compare the street name signs overhead and across the street (see "Seattle Street Signs").

SEATTLE STREET SIGNS

The top of the Newell stairs (3) is a good place to view two street sign styles curious urban hikers might want to know about. The "W NEWELL ST." sign above your head shows a walking man next to the street name. According to SDOT's website, this icon indicates a "pedestrian facility." What's significant for stairway searchers is that this icon is gradually being added to all street name signs wherever the right-of-way consists of stairs.

Across the street, the sign "10 TH AVE W" is brown instead of the usual green. According to the City, this indicates a street that is either maintained by the parks department or that's part of the historic Olmsted boulevard system. Interestingly, 10th Avenue/Queen Anne Boulevard doesn't exactly fit either criterion. While the parks department maintains the plantings on either side, SDOT is actually responsible for the street, and Queen Anne Boulevard isn't part of the original Olmsted-designed boulevard plan.

Street name signs across the city will be replaced by 2016, using funds from the voter-approved "Bridging the Gap" levy (many stairways are being refurbished or repaired using these funds). All new signs will follow federal standards for size and reflectivity, and will include the special icons and the coloring.

From the top of the Newell stairs, turn left onto 10th Avenue W. As you walk north a short block to W Armour Street, start looking on your left for the top of the next stairs. As you get close, the stairway handrails get screened from view by the trunk of a beautiful cedar tree. Take the Armour stairs down (there's a street sign at the head of the stairs).

To Views and the Ruffner Stairs (17 steps up, 156 steps down): Immediately at the bottom of the Armour stairs, turn right (north) onto 10th Place W, a charming, narrow lane. After one block, cross W Fulton Street on the right side, so you can climb the 17 steps up to the elevated sidewalk along 10th Place W. As you walk along, you'll pass several stairways connecting your sidewalk with the street below. Once you reach W Barrett Street, take the 16 stairs back down to the intersection at street level.

Cross W Barrett Street and continue up what has now become 10th Avenue W. The houses are a bit more eclectic and not as captivating, but here you're walking along the top of a ridge, with nice views to either side.

When you reach the next intersection, you'll see W Etruria Street on the right and W Dravus Street on the left. Turn left onto Dravus, which is essentially just a driveway ending in a sidewalk. Follow the sidewalk until you reach a short stretch of 18 stairs, which end just short of 11th Avenue W. Turn right onto the sidewalk, which takes you toward a lane running above and parallel to 11th Avenue.

This lane/driveway eventually merges back with 11th Avenue, just before coming to W Bertona Street. Turn left onto the sidewalk that runs above W Bertona, on the south side. At the next block take the 15 stairs heading back down to street level and cross over to the northeast corner of W Bertona and 12th Avenue W. From here if you turn to look kitty-corner to the south, you get a surprisingly good view of Alki Point jutting into the Sound, with Elliott Bay in the foreground.

Turn right onto 13th Avenue W, again taking a sidewalk above the east side of the street, which ascends slightly before cresting and turning downhill. At the crest, you can look ahead to the ridge beyond the Ship Canal, with glimpses of Ballard to the left and Phinney Ridge to the right. Just a couple of houses beyond the crest, look left across the street to see Fishermen's Terminal. Even farther west, beyond Salmon Bay and the Hiram M. Chittenden Locks, you can see the railroad drawbridge across the Ship Canal (provided it's in the up position).

Soon you'll be able to look down toward the Ruffner stairs, ahead on the left. As you near W Ruffner Street, still on the sidewalk above street level, note the striking home ahead. A view tower dominates the house on one side, clad in what looks like pleasingly rusted steel. The tall roof slopes down to a set of huge windows running around the top, with what looks to be dynamite views north and west.

At the corner of 13th and Ruffner, take the 22 stairs down to the street. Then turn left and head across 13th to the Ruffner stairs (4). They were refurbished in 2007, reducing the number of steps from 135 to 85. **WWW** The stairway now has double-rail handrails and other newer features, but in some places the steps reveal their true vintage. For instance, look for the double-stacked concrete slabs the city repurposed as stairway treads when the old streetcar tracks were removed, back in the 1940s.

Overland Trek to the Prosch Walkway: At the bottom of the Ruffner stairs, turn left onto the sidewalk at 14th Avenue W. At the next block turn left onto W Bertona Street, then right onto 13th Avenue W.

Continue south on 13th Avenue W. On the right as you approach the next street, you might catch an unusual sight for a residential neighborhood: what looks like a very modern house, with roll-up glass garage doors topped by a peaked, glass-faced gable. On the face of the gable is a large, vivid red insignia with "20" inside a circle. Fire Station 20 is more than fifty-five years old and very small, with room for only one engine. It also doesn't meet current earthquake standards for fire stations, so a new, bigger structure along 15th Avenue is expected to replace it by 2014.

Route's end, looking back at the Boston stairs

Just past the fire station, carefully cross W Dravus Street, a busy arterial. Head slightly uphill on 13th and at the next street turn right, onto W Barrett Street, then left onto Prosch Avenue W.

About eight houses in, Prosch Avenue starts a slow, semicircular curve. At the top of the curve, turn left up a driveway, just past a street sign for W Armour Street. Walk toward the mysterious, laurel-shrouded opening just left of the driveway. This is the public Prosch walkway (5). **WWW**

Completing the Loop at the Boston Stairs (93 steps down): When you reach the far end of the Prosch walkway, you'll be facing 13th Ave W. Cross and turn left onto the far sidewalk, following it around the complex intersection ahead. The sidewalk starts out heading northeast but hairpins south to follow 12th Avenue W.

Walk along 12th Avenue, first straight south and then along an S curve as 12th becomes W Bothwell Street. The road then curves back south, ending up as 13th Avenue W.

Shortly after the S curve, 13th Avenue splits, with a median running down the middle. Take the left-hand lane, which runs slightly above the other lane. You'll pass the next street, W Wheeler Street, downhill from your earlier encounter (you're also passing some unexplored flights of Wheeler stairs on either side). Just before you reach Gilman Drive W, you'll see a median between Gilman and a parking lot on the left. Walk up the parking lot, a few feet removed from the active arterial street.

At the end of the parking lot, you run out of sidewalk, so carefully cross Gilman here. On the other side head left, toward your final stairway.

When you reach the Boston stairs (6) on your right, take them down. These stairs are spectacular in the fall. At the bottom of the first flight you'll cross the upper lane of 13th Avenue. Continue on a shorter flight to the lower lane of 13th at W Boston Street, and you've arrived near your starting point.

At the bottom of the stairs, look for the whimsical animal prints someone placed in fresh concrete on the street. Also look for a nearby plaque indicating that these stairs were constructed by the WPA in 1940. **WWW**

13 South Magnolia

It's easy to get the impression that this neighborhood is just a subdued enclave of expensive homes with big views across the Sound. That's true for the part most accessible to visitors in cars, where Magnolia Boulevard runs along the western edge of the bluff. But there's a lot more in Magnolia to excite a curious visitor's interest. This stairway walk traverses the entire peninsula, where you'll explore the breadth of Magnolia's homes and architecture, its contours and views.

There are two glacially deposited hills sitting on top of Magnolia Bluff, with Pleasant Valley running in between. This up-and-down topography creates opportunities for fine stairways and views. The route starts at Magnolia Park, where so many visitors come, and continues down the Glenmont stairs to isolated Perkins Lane. Here you'll view many impressive homes built just above the water, right at the base of this notoriously unstable bluff.

Terrific Puget Sound view from Montavista Place

You won't tempt fate too long before heading back up the gracefully decrepit Montavista stairs and away from the bluff. You'll visit more stairways and take in the beautiful homes and views of the western ridge of Magnolia, before dipping across Pleasant Valley and then up a long stairway stashed away on the flanks of the eastern ridge. You'll climb up and back down the hill, then meander south along the eastern portion of Magnolia, before reaching Ella Bailey Park, with its awesome views of Queen Anne and Downtown. Your walk ends near "the Village," the charmingly compact retail hub of the neighborhood. Here you can wind down at the local pub or one of several cafes.

Length:	**4.5 miles**
Walking Time:	2 hours 20 minutes
Steps Down:	327
Steps Up:	405
Kid-Friendly:	Although this is one of the longest stairway walks, you could take a fun, truncated walk to kid-centric and view-rich Ella Bailey Park from the Village area, via W McGraw and 28th Avenue W. The only stairs would be at the Ella Bailey end, where there's a drinking fountain and portable toilet.
Cafes/Pubs:	This walk begins and ends at Magnolia Village, the neighborhood's small retail district. You'll find a pub, coffee shops, and restaurants up and down W McGraw Street.

Getting There: If driving, park on W McGraw west of 35th Avenue, where two-hour parking restrictions don't apply. Metro Transit Route 24 (from Downtown Seattle) and MT31 (Fremont and U District) both stop at W McGraw and 35th; MT31 doesn't run Sundays.

To the Glenmont Stairs and Perkins Lane (203 steps down): You'll take the longest stairway, the Glenmont stairs, early in the walk. These steps lead down to Perkins Lane, which runs along the bottom of the bluff below Magnolia Boulevard.

From W McGraw Street, head south on 35th Avenue W to the first major right, Viewmont Way W. Continue southwest on Viewmont, which curves right just before Constance Drive W joins in from the left. Take the next left onto Constance, a lane turning sharply right downhill as it detaches from Viewmont. Turn left from Constance at the next street, Montavista Place W.

From here it's a quick drop down Montavista to Magnolia Boulevard, which you'll need to carefully cross without benefit of a crosswalk. At the far side, turn right and head up the sidewalk. From here you'll enjoy views out over Elliott Bay. Below you, out of sight at the bottom of the bluff, is Perkins Lane, your next destination.

As you walk west along the top of the bluff, watch for the magnificent madrona trees, their pistachio-colored trunks peeking out from peeling red-orange bark. It's said that this neighborhood's name derives from the 1790s, when Captain George Vancouver mistakenly noted these trees in his ship's log as magnolias.

You'll continue along Magnolia Boulevard for two blocks. Just where you can see the road curving up to the right ahead of you, look for the handrails of your first stairway peeking up from the downslope on the left. This will be just opposite where W Glenmont Lane descends to meet Magnolia Boulevard from

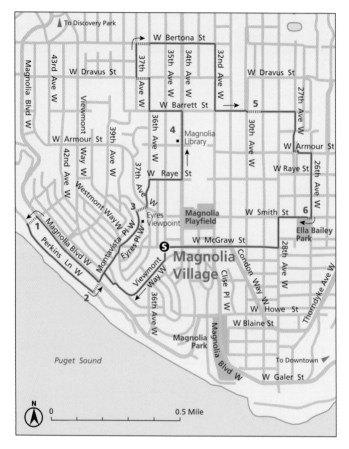

the hill above. The Glenmont stairway (1) is 203 steps, according to the city. We counted 202, probably within the margin of counting error. The first 130 steps (or so) are wood; the remainder are concrete.

At the bottom of the stairs, turn left onto Perkins Lane. Walking along Perkins, it's easy to envy the homeowners' incredible views of the Sound and Elliott Bay. But you'll also see megatons of unstable hill towering above these houses, with massive steel and concrete walls trying to stave off the ongoing slippage as long as possible. You can see and hear the water squeezing out of the slope!

HISTORY PLUS TOPOGRAPHY EQUALS AMBIENCE

From its earliest development until now, Magnolia has been "a peninsula apart" from the rest of the city. The Ship Canal, to the north, and two dozen sets of Burlington Northern tracks, to the west, isolate Magnolia, much like the Duwamish River and Puget Ridge isolate West Seattle. Because of this separation from the rest of Seattle, Magnolia grew more slowly than other neighborhoods. Development didn't get underway in earnest until after the Dravus Street Bridge opened in 1931; by comparison, almost half the homes in more centrally located Capitol Hill were already built by 1940.

Magnolia is almost wholly residential, with construction there happening in two major waves. The first one hit just after World War II, when demand for modestly priced family homes drove a home-building boom on moderately sloped sites, mostly in and around Pleasant Valley. Here the homes tend to be smaller and more cozily "yard-centric," with thoughtfully tended DIY landscaping. In the 1960s, the market shifted to a more upscale buyer. You'll see much pricier homes near the south bluff along Magnolia Boulevard, and atop a few other ridges. They tend to be much larger, and to place equal emphasis on architectural style as well as taking advantage of the views.

The architecture feels harmonious within each individual section of Magnolia, but you can't walk far without moving into a different part of the neighborhood with another look and feel. For the neighborhood explorer, there's a unique ambience here: varied and interesting, yet always calm and peaceful.

Montavista Stairs to Magnolia Library (154 steps up): As you stroll along Perkins Lane, you'll eventually come to a slight rise with concrete traffic barriers at the top. Here on the left, you'll see the Montavista stairs (2).

These stairs have been heavily impacted by the movement of the slope underneath them. As you go up, you'll notice that the rise and run of the steps varies, and the line of the stairs wavers back and forth. It's not clear to us how much longer these stairs can remain open without extensive rebuilding. Be ready to alter your route depending on conditions when you go!

At the top, head left for a few feet on the sidewalk next to Magnolia Boulevard until you come even with Montavista Place W. At that point, cross Magnolia and start back up Montavista, toward the Magnolia Library.

Finding your way is easy at first as you walk straight up Montavista Place, but soon you'll come to a seven-way intersection with a triangular patch of grass in the middle. Here's how to keep it simple: stay on the right sidewalk along Montavista; when it arrives at the intersection, turn right to cross the next street over (Westmont). This has you temporarily walking up the right-hand sidewalk on Westmont until you reach the next part of the intersection. Here, take a soft right to get back onto Montavista; a hard right will put you onto W McGraw. From there, continue up Montavista; you've made it through the intersection, no problem!

When Montavista starts curving to the left, watch for the next street, Eyres Place W, which comes in from the right (3). You'll continue past Eyres, but it's a great spot to pause for an outstanding view of Elliott Bay, the ship terminals, and on a clear day, Mount Rainier.

Keep walking on Montavista Place W as it continues its leftward curve. Just as you can see Montavista start climbing more sharply to the left up ahead,

The Montavista "Moving Stairs"

watch for an unsigned lane heading downhill to your right, and take it when you see it. This short lane ends at a skewed four-way junction; take a soft left, which puts you onto 36th Avenue W (a hard left puts you onto 37th).

Stay on 36th, heading generally north, until you reach the next street, W Raye. Turn right onto Raye, and begin your first descent into Pleasant Valley. Take the second left onto 34th Avenue W. One long block later, as you reach W Armour, you'll see Magnolia Library (4) ahead on the left. It's beautiful inside and well worth a quick visit.

MAGNIFICENT MAGNOLIA LIBRARY

In 1943, Magnolia's first library opened at the site of a former tavern in the Village. This only happened after years of local community advocacy, during which Magnolia was served by a bookmobile or, during the budget-cutting Depression years, by driving over to Queen Anne or Ballard (no public transportation was available for a book run). After several moves from one temporary site to another, this library was built and opened in 1964.

The architect, Paul Hayden Kirk (1914–1995), was a leading pioneer of Pacific Northwest Modernism. You'll see that style expressed here: generous use of natural materials, a clean geometrical design and a harmony with the building's outside surroundings. Kirk's style can also be seen at the Intiman Theater, the Odegaard Undergraduate Library at the University of Washington, and University Unitarian Church in Wedgwood.

As you approach Magnolia Library (4), you aren't bowled over by its scale: it fits comfortably on its slope, overlooking Pleasant Valley through large windows. The exterior is wood and glass, put together in a way that manages to be simple, arresting, and inviting all at the same time—perfectly in tune with Magnolia neighborhood as a whole. At the front, along 34th Avenue, there's a beautiful, curving entry staircase. WWW

The interior is mostly wood, with substantial open beams filling the space above. WWW The furniture is wood too, expressly designed for this building by American Craft movement luminary George Nakashima (1905–1990). Nakashima was born in Spokane, but like most Japanese citizens on the West Coast, he spent World War II at internment camps. There he met an influential teacher and honed his abilities in traditional Japanese carpentry and woodworking. Trained originally as an architect, Nakashima's philosophy is reflected in the beautiful chairs and tables that fill the library: "Furniture is like architecture only on a different scale. I'm happy working small."

Across the Peninsula via Pleasant Valley (212 steps up, 99 steps down): This next part of the route traverses the Magnolia peninsula, from one hill to the other. First you'll climb the western hill, then dip down into Pleasant Valley before heading back up the eastern hill via the Barrett stairs.

From Magnolia Library, continue north along 34th Avenue, turning left on the next block at W Barrett Street. Just before turning left, take a rightward look toward the sweeping, acorn-like profile of Our Lady of Fatima church halfway down the block. `WWW` This building was designed for his own parish by architect James Klontz, working in what's considered to be an "organic" style of Northwest Modernism. It was completed in 1968.

As you walk west up Barrett, you'll again be climbing the westernmost hill of Magnolia. After two blocks on Barrett, turn right onto 36th Avenue W and walk one block north to W Dravus Street. To your left, Dravus continues as a stairway up the hill, and up you go. `WWW` At the midpoint, you'll cross an alley before heading up a final flight.

At the top, turn right onto 37th Avenue and walk two blocks, first passing W Prosper Street on the left before arriving at W Bertona Street. Here, Bertona plunges downhill in the form of stairs, disappearing mysteriously into a tunnel of trees. `WWW` It finally opens onto 36th Avenue W, where you'll continue straight ahead on Bertona all the way to 32nd Avenue W.

Turn right onto 32nd and walk two blocks, turning left onto W Barrett Street. From here, walk east on Barrett as you begin to climb the easternmost hill of Magnolia. You'll notice the street ending in stairs two blocks ahead, at 30th Avenue W. These stairs (5) are quite nice, set back unobtrusively from the street. `WWW` Be careful about crossing over to them, as 30th is a busy conduit into and out of Magnolia via the nearby Dravus Street Bridge.

You'll discover that the stairway is even more unobtrusive and easy to miss at the upper end, opening onto a shared driveway well back from the street. `WWW` Continue straight ahead on Barrett until you reach 27th Avenue W, where you'll turn right.

To Ella Bailey Park and Views (25 steps down, 39 steps up): After one block on 27th, the street makes a slight jog before continuing south. Here at the southeast corner there's a great view of Queen Anne over a vacant lot. Continue south one more block to W Armour Street, where you'll turn left to walk down 25 stairs. At the bottom continue straight ahead one block east, then turn right onto 26th Avenue W.

Walk three blocks south on 26th, to W Smith Street. To your right, Smith Street continues upward as stairs. At the top is Ella Bailey Park (6), with a large play structure, skateboard-friendly concrete walls, expansive areas of grass, and fabulous views. You can take in Queen Anne, the Space Needle, Downtown and Elliott Bay, and even Mount Rainier, when conditions allow. `WWW`

Ella Bailey Park was opened in 2007. It had been the asphalt playground area for Magnolia Elementary School, but after the school was shuttered it fell into disrepair. The Pro Parks Levy contributed $1.4 million to revive this spot as a friendly neighborhood hangout and favorite New Year's Eve and July 4th fireworks viewpoint.

To Magnolia Village: After taking in the views at Ella Bailey Park, walk west on W Smith Street to 28th Avenue W, and turn left. Continue south on 28th Avenue. You'll be walking alongside mothballed Magnolia School WWW until you reach W McGraw Street on your left. McGraw makes a big jog here, so keep walking another 20 yards or so until you reach the

western continuation of McGraw on the right. Here you'll see a crosswalk that will take you safely across 28th Avenue and then west on McGraw.

After three blocks on McGraw, you'll cross Condon Way W. You'll be in the Magnolia Village area then, fast approaching your starting place.

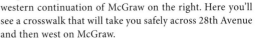

14 The Olmsted Vision: The Arboretum, Interlaken Park, and Volunteer Park

In 1903 the City of Seattle commissioned the prominent Olmsted Brothers firm of landscape architects to design a system of parks for Seattle. After a month-long visit here from Boston, John C. Olmsted made recommendations that deeply shape the character and unique livability of Seattle today.

He envisioned a grand 20-mile boulevard from the shore of Lake Washington all the way to Puget Sound, with parks and playgrounds interspersed along the way. Well after that first visit, Olmsted and his successor, James Dawson, continued to work out the details. On this walk you'll touch on significant landmarks of the lengthy relationship between Olmsted and Seattle, from Olmsted's early recommendation for a view tower in Volunteer Park to Dawson's General Plan for Washington Park Arboretum, completed in 1936.

Parks, history, neighborhoods, architecture, stairways—this walk has it all. You'll explore an important segment of Olmsted's splendid boulevard vision, along a string of parks: The Arboretum, Interlaken Park, and Volunteer Park, located in the Montlake, Stevens, and Broadway neighborhoods, respectively. You'll also see many examples of the vibrant residential architecture that was created for a prospering middle and upper class in the early decades of the twentieth century. You'll encounter magnificent stairways, such as the unique

Volunteer Park reservoir

hand-hewn stone stairs inside Interlaken Park, and the 106 steel stairs that spiral up a narrow space inside the Volunteer Park Water Tower, toward panoramic views of the Seattle skyline.

Length:	**4.2 miles**
Walking Time:	2 hours
Steps Down:	243
Steps Up:	359
Kid-Friendly:	At 4 miles, this walk is probably too long for younger kids, but a workable adaptation of the walk could center around Volunteer Park and the water tower.
Cafes/Pubs:	Volunteer Park Cafe, a neighborhood institution in Capitol Hill (midway through the walk), is great for lunch or a snack. Several wonderful cafes and restaurants can be found four blocks south of Volunteer Park on 15th Avenue E just beyond Roy Street. Near the start/end of the walk, between the Arboretum and Interlaken Park, likely places along 24th Avenue E include Fuel Coffee, Mont's Market (with a small deli), Montlake Ale House, and the Italian restaurant Cafe Lago (dinner only).

Getting There: If driving, park along E McGraw Street between 24th Avenue E and the Arboretum. Look carefully at the signs, as this residential area has permit parking. You should be fine most daytime hours but parking here is outlawed altogether several times a year, mostly on University of Washington football game days. Metro Transit 43 bus from Downtown stops at this junction on the way to the University District. MT 48 stops here as well; it goes between Mount Baker and Loyal Heights, running through Capitol Hill, the University District, Ravenna, and Greenwood.

WASHINGTON PARK ARBORETUM

By 1896, the Puget Mill Company had completely logged the land where today's Washington Park Arboretum and adjoining Broadmoor golf and residential development are located. In 1900, to further its plans for the logged-off land, the company gave 62 acres to the City in return for a water supply to an adjoining future development (Broadmoor). Although Seattle now has over 400 parks and open spaces, in 1900 there were only three: Kinnear, Volunteer, and Denny parks. This swap created the core of a fourth, Washington Park. The rest of the park's eventual 230 acres were pieced together in a flurry of purchases and grants between 1900 and 1904.

When John C. Olmsted made his transformative visit to Seattle in May 1903, he included Washington Park in his vision of a 20-mile-long system of parks and green boulevards running from Lake Washington to the Sound. Then in 1924 the City passed a resolution designating Washington Park as a university arboretum. Work on the Arboretum advanced only slowly into the Depression but picked up in December 1935, when 300 federal WPA workers were suddenly assigned to the project. The Olmsted firm's James Dawson caught up to this new development a few months later with a general plan for the Washington Arboretum, and work ramped up considerably after that.

Today the Arboretum land is owned and maintained by Seattle Parks, while the collection of more than 10,000 plants and 4,400 plant species is maintained by the University of Washington Botanic Gardens.

Although this walk just grazes the western border, you can easily spend a full day wandering throughout the Arboretum, in any season. WWW A visitor center, where you can learn about its many attractions, is located at the north end. There are kayaking and canoeing opportunities on that end as well. On the south side there's a fee-for-entry Japanese garden, plus the newest addition to the Arboretum's collection, the Pacific Connections Garden. The bulk of the Arboretum contains numerous gardens and plant collections, served by dozens of winding trails.

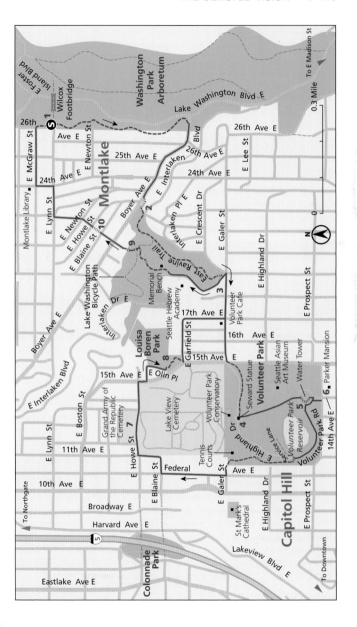

Arboretum Stroll: You'll walk briefly along the western edge of the Washington Park Arboretum before heading west along the southern border of the Montlake neighborhood. To begin head east on E McGraw Street until it ends at the Arboretum. Here, turn right and follow the sidewalk south, skirting a small play area.

As you pass the play area, glance left at the footbridge (1). It's an excellent entrance point to the central axis of the park, should you want to embark on further explorations of the Arboretum. The bridge, known as the Wilcox Footbridge or "Sewer Trestle," is a Seattle Landmark. It was built in 1911 to carry sewer lines over Lake Washington Boulevard to the Broadmoor residential development and golf course.

Once you've passed the play area, the sidewalk turns into packed gravel. It continues along the west edge of the Arboretum, now threading beneath trees and tall conifers. In less than 0.25 mile, you'll see a traffic light through the shrubs ahead, where Boyer Avenue E runs into Lake Washington Boulevard from the right. Just before the intersection, take a branch of the path curving up to the right. After a few steps, the path turns into a sidewalk alongside Boyer, and you enter the residential part of the Montlake neighborhood.

Follow Boyer Avenue past the traffic circle at 25th Avenue E. When you reach a crosswalk signal at 24th Avenue E, cross over from the south side of Boyer, to position yourself for the stairs coming up on your left.

To Interlaken Park (129 steps up): When you pull even with Boyer Children's Clinic across the street, turn away from Boyer Avenue and up a set of 26 stairs (2). **WWW** They top out in a cul-de-sac where E Interlaken Boulevard and 21st Avenue E meet. To the right, Interlaken Boulevard continues as a broad paved pedestrian/bicycle lane, closed to auto traffic as it enters Interlaken Park. The boulevard here in the park is known as the Lake Washington Bicycle Path (see "Interlaken Park and the Historic Lake Washington Bicycle Path"). Turn right to head into the park. **WWW**

About 0.1 mile into the park, Interlaken Boulevard/Lake Washington Bicycle Path makes a hairpin right turn, crossing a ravine with a seasonally flowing creek. At this point you'll turn away from Interlaken Boulevard to head up the west side of the ravine on a dirt path (shown on map as "East Ravine Trail"). A wood-and-wire fence stands alongside the path between you and the bottom of the ravine. **WWW**

Follow the footpath up the ravine through the eastern section of Interlaken Park. In winter the views down to the creek and across the ravine are unobstructed by trees, but in other seasons the ambience can be very different, with birds singing and frogs cheeping somewhere among the shadows and deep-green foliage.

As you near the top of the ravine, continue past a path with stairs that climbs up to your right. Soon after, your path will zig left and quickly hairpin right, with 56 timber steps to climb before the path levels out somewhat.

INTERLAKEN PARK AND THE HISTORIC LAKE WASHINGTON BICYCLE PATH

In the 1890s bicycles underwent two major design changes that made them wildly popular. Pneumatic rubber tires made the ride comfortable on cobblestone streets, and the introduction of gearing and flywheels made it possible to go reasonably fast without having pedals directly attached to a huge, clumsy front or rear wheel. By the late 1890s Seattle had about 10,000 bicycles but, aside from a few cobblestone streets, very few places to ride.

In response, city engineer and future mayor George Cotterill proposed a 25-mile system of bicycle-friendly recreational trails, which later became the foundation of the Olmsted firm's boulevard and park system for Seattle. A 10-mile stretch of cinder path was opened between Lake Union and Lake Washington in 1897. Part of that original path, on Interlaken Boulevard between Delmar Drive and 24th Avenue, is now the Lake Washington Bicycle Path, a Seattle Landmark.

In 1903, the Olmsted firm recommended that land surrounding this path be purchased to create a park. Between 1905 and 1970, twenty-seven separate purchases were made to create Interlaken Park as it exists today.

Keep going until the path is blocked by a large maple tree, creating a T intersection. Turn left here, and head up 38 more timber stairs until you reach the street above (Interlaken Drive E, which you'll return to). Next you'll visit the third of Olmsted's parks, Volunteer Park. On the way there and back you'll explore the Stevens neighborhood and North Capitol Hill, passing many 1900s-era architectural treasures, some of them small and quaint, others more stately and monumental.

Take the crosswalk straight ahead, across Interlaken Drive E, then turn right onto E Galer Street and into the Stevens neighborhood (3).

Stevens Neighborhood: From here to Volunteer Park, the character of the walk changes dramatically again. You'll walk through a neighborhood of picturesque homes, built in the early 1900s for an emerging middle class that prospered during the Klondike Gold Rush. These houses represent a spectrum of styles: Tudor Revival, Queen Anne, Bungalow, Classic Box, and English Cottage.

After you turn onto E Galer Street, you'll immediately pass Stevens Elementary School (1906) on your left. At 18th Avenue E, you can take a short detour to the left to view its Colonial Revival facade. This school is named after Isaac Stevens, Washington's first territorial governor (1853). **WWW**

At the next block, on the northwest corner of E Galer and 17th Avenue E, is Volunteer Park Cafe. The building, situated in the middle of this residential neighborhood, enjoyed a lengthy previous life as a grocery.

To the Volunteer Park Conservatory: After just a half-dozen blocks, E Galer Street comes to an end at 15th Avenue E, with E Highland Drive continuing into the park, just ahead. Across 15th Avenue to the right is historic Lake View Cemetery, behind a tall chainlink fence and a line of pampas grass. Here lie several of Seattle's founding luminaries: Asa Mercer, Doc Maynard, Henry Yesler, and David Denny. Other permanent residents include Princess Angeline, daughter of the city's namesake, Chief Sealth; Nordstrom founder John W.; poet Denise Levertov; and actor and martial artist Bruce Lee.

Cross 15th Avenue E to the Volunteer Park entrance and a paved footpath. The path runs along Highland Drive across the north end of the park toward the Volunteer Park Conservatory. Walk past several side-paths on the left to reach the statue of William Seward standing in the middle of a traffic circle in front of the conservatory. As Abraham Lincoln's secretary of state, Seward bought the Alaska Territory from the Russians for $7.2 million—known at the time as "Seward's Folly."

Poke your head into the Volunteer Park Conservatory (4), a fascinating place. **WWW** A donation is requested, though an admission fee is under consideration and may be in effect as you read this. Built in 1912, the conservatory is a Victorian-style greenhouse, modeled after the Crystal Palace in London. It contains more than 6000 square feet of public viewing area, with a lot more behind-the-scenes space for maintaining the public displays. All of it is under the care of Seattle Parks horticulturalists.

Volunteer Park Water Tower (119 steps up and down): Follow Mr. Seward's visionary gaze away from the conservatory, walking south along a tree-lined lane. As you emerge into a parking area you'll see the Seattle Asian Art Museum, a fine Art Deco building that faces Volunteer Park Reservoir to your right. Also on the right, overlooking the reservoir and the Space Needle in the distance, is a glossy black sculpture, *Black Sun*, created in 1969 by Isamu Noguchi out of Brazilian granite.

Walk straight ahead toward the Volunteer Park Water Tower, which stands at the park's highest point. **WWW** It was first envisioned in Olmsted's 1903 plan, in which he suggested an observation tower for a city view. Take the path up to its north entrance. Inside, start up the narrow, spiraling steel staircase (5). **WWW**

At the top of the tower, 75 feet above its base, you'll have wonderful views of the park and the city. **WWW** There's also an extensive display about the Olmsted firm's huge contribution to the look and feel of today's Seattle. A helpful web document on the Olmsted legacy can be seen at www.ci.seattle.wa.us /friendsofolmstedparks.

To the Parker Mansion and North through the Park (30 steps down, 13 steps up): In the early 1900s, "Millionaires Row" was developed just south

A view from the top of Volunteer Park Water Tower

of Volunteer Park as an exclusive enclave for Seattle's "nouveau richest." A grand specimen of the type is located just steps away from the water tower. As you head down the south tower entrance steps, walk toward the park exit. Across the street and to the left, at 1409 E Prospect, is a 1909 Neoclassical Revival mansion (6) built by colorful stockbroker George Parker. **WWW** This mansion is monumental, with more than thirty rooms, five covered porches, and seven fireplaces, and it's a designated Seattle Landmark. Mr. Parker earned much of his riches selling bogus stock in a nonexistent company. For that he went to federal prison, just one year after moving into the mansion. He was later found not guilty, on account of ignorance, and pardoned.

From the park exit, double back toward the tower steps and turn left onto the sidewalk, next to the drive encircling the tower. As you approach the reservoir, the drive divides. Take the sidewalk alongside the left branch of the drive. As the sidewalk goes around the circular reservoir, it moves close to E Prospect Street before withdrawing to the north.

Soon after the concrete sidewalk changes to a gravel path, look for a small service lane to the right, angling up and away from the drive along the reservoir slope. This service lane is your landmark for a set of hard-to-see stairs dropping away from the path on your left. There's no railing, just a flat concrete landing before the stairs head down. If you pass the service lane without seeing the stairs, turn back to look again!

After stepping down these 30 stairs, turn right onto a dirt path. You're aiming for the obscure northwest corner of Volunteer Park, where you'll make your exit. Keep on this path until you reach a three-way junction. The left branch heads down to a bordering street; take the right branch, a broader, somewhat rocky path, up a small grade. In a few steps the path splits again; again, take the right branch, which leads up to a small set of 13 stairs.

At the top of the stairs, turn left onto a wide gravel path, which passes some tennis courts on the right. At the distant corner of the tennis courts, just beyond a drinking fountain, follow the path downhill to the left. Soon this path turns to asphalt, takes a hairpin turn out of Volunteer Park, and descends the west end of E Galer Street.

Continue a few steps on E Galer to its intersection with Federal Avenue E. Kitty-corner to the right is the Perry B. Truax Residence, a notable Tudor Revival home. Ahead of you, a block to the west up Galer, Saint Mark's Cathedral commands the west slope of Capitol Hill, looking down on I-5 and Lake Union.

To the GAR Cemetery and Louisa Boren Park: Turn right onto Federal Avenue and walk north, passing fancy houses right and left until you reach E Blaine Street. This is the same Blaine that hosts one of the longest stairways in Seattle, just a few blocks west (see walk 9, "Eastlake, North Capitol Hill, and Portage Bay"). Turn right onto E Blaine, which goes a scant block before it ends with a 90-degree turn to the left, onto 11th Avenue E.

Continue north on 11th Avenue for one block, skirting the northwest corner of Lake View Cemetery, hidden behind tall hedges on your right. At the next block turn right, onto E Howe Street (home to the Howe stairs, also in walk 9). As Howe curves slightly uphill, you'll be walking between Lake View Cemetery on the right and what appears to be a park on the left. A shallow horseshoe-shaped driveway will lead you into the Grand Army of the Republic (GAR) Cemetery, where more than 526 Civil War veterans and their spouses are buried (7). **WWW**

Stay on E Howe until you reach 15th Avenue E. Cross 15th Avenue at the crosswalk, then turn right and walk south on 15th, turning left at the next block, onto E Olin Place. E Olin is just a short dogleg of a street that ends up back at 15th, but it has beautifully tended homes that look across a long ravine to Lake Washington. Just as E Olin rejoins 15th Avenue E, you'll see the Louisa Boren Park sign on your left.

Louisa Boren Park (8) is named for the last survivor of Seattle's founding Denny family. It covers more than 7 acres, most of it a thickly wooded ravine that continues down to Interlaken Park. The upper end of the park, here at the corner of Olin and 15th, features killer views north, to the Union Bay Natural Area and the neighborhood of Laurelhurst (see walk 6, "Laurelhurst"). **WWW** You can also glimpse Lake Washington beyond.

Behind you are darkly weathered, hulking steel sculptures by Lee Kelly, commissioned by the Seattle Arts Commission and installed in 1975. Monumental as they are, they fit in with the massive trees and add a brooding calm to the scene. **WWW** If you're not into brooding, this is a very pleasant space, with plenty of nice spots to take in the views.

To Interlaken Boulevard (94 steps down): From Louisa Boren Park, turn east (left) onto E Garfield Street and walk downhill four blocks, past a number of interesting front yards, then turn right onto 17th Avenue E. Walk south for a long block, and you'll arrive at E Galer Street and back at the Volunteer Park Cafe. Turn left and walk two blocks east along E Galer. Just after passing Stevens Elementary, this time on your right, you'll reach the familiar five-way intersection at the southern tip of Interlaken Park. Take a hard left onto Interlaken Drive E. From here you'll return through Interlaken Park, tracking farther to the west this time.

Follow Interlaken Drive as it winds gently downhill. Unlike the stretch of carless Interlaken Boulevard you walked on before, Interlaken Drive is open to autos. There's a narrow dirt path on the right side of the curb to separate you from the sparse traffic. After a few twists and turns on Interlaken Drive, you'll see the impressive Seattle Hebrew Academy coming up on your left. **WWW** Just where you pull even with the main building and its large portico, look for a broad gravel path angling from the street to your right and down into the trees.

Leaving Interlaken Drive here, follow your spur path as it heads northeast to join the main trail. About 50 yards along, take a quick detour down a short set of timber steps to the right, flanked by a fence on either side. At the bottom, turn left toward a viewing area with a columnar-basalt bench, sculpted by John Hoge. **WWW** The bench memorializes Rob Reed, a KCTS TV producer who died on assignment at age thirty-eight; he often ran through this lovely spot in the park. One side of the bench is polished smooth; the other half is rough, with four maple leaves polished into the sitting surface.

As you leave the memorial bench, you'll rejoin the main path. A dozen feet beyond that, the path branches; take the right branch. Soon you'll encounter 28 timber steps followed by a T intersection blocked by a wooden fence, with Interlaken Boulevard visible below. Turn right here, and this time you'll encounter 26 hewn stone steps on the way down to Interlaken Boulevard (9). **WWW** Watch where you put your feet, as their dimensions vary widely!

At Interlaken Boulevard, cross over, angling slightly left, to meet the gravel path on the other side. Continue immediately down more stone steps, 28 in all. The path curves and then branches; take the left branch as you continue downhill. Soon you'll come to a set of 12 timber steps curving out of Interlaken Park to deposit you on 22nd Avenue E.

To the 22nd Avenue Stairs and Back (107 steps up): Head north on 22nd Avenue past Boyer Avenue E, continuing another block to E Blaine Street.

Up the 22nd Avenue stairs to Howe Street

Here you'll encounter your last stairway: the 107 steps connecting Blaine with Howe (10). When you arrive at the top of the stairs, continue straight on 22nd Avenue past E Newton Street, angling left (north) toward E Lynn Street.

At the intersection of E Lynn and 22nd, marked by a traffic circle, look kitty-corner left to where the notable Craftsman-style Mauss Residence sits on a small rise. **WWW** Featured in *Bungalow* magazine in 1916, it's an exemplar of Seattle Craftsman style, with deep eaves and a shingled exterior.

Turn right onto E Lynn and continue downhill; be careful not to make a hard right here, which will put you on 23rd Avenue E. At the bottom of Lynn, turn left onto busy 24th Avenue E. Continue down the block to the traffic light at E McGraw Street, where you'll be able to safely cross 24th back to your starting spot.

15 Downtown: City Hall to Pike Place

This stairway walk makes a terrific "city day," either as a Downtown refresher course for Seattleites, or an off-the-beaten-path alternative for visitors.

Among many architectural treats, you'll visit buildings from Seattle's brief but spectacular Art Deco period; peer up the bulging side of a nationally acclaimed Postmodern-style tower; and get a close-up view of one of the few remaining buildings that went up right after the Great Fire of 1889. This walk reveals architectural details that are easy to miss from a car or bus: tusked walrus heads glaring; Indian faces gazing; lilliputian figures strolling down walls and along ceilings; a shiny chrome arrow buried deep in a boulder. You'll see intricate architectural allusions to early commerce in the Pacific Northwest, and inspect quirky sidewalk hatch-cover art.

This route keeps mostly inside the West Edge district between Pike Place Market and Pioneer Square, edging along the Waterfront area to the west and the retail core to the east. It starts near the striking Rem Koolhaas–designed Central Library, heads south to visit the grand staircase of City Hall, then turns north toward the busy and beautiful Harbor Steps, with nods to several historic buildings along the way. It continues via multiple stairways and passages as far as Pike Place Market, before turning back toward the starting point. Highlights on the back stretch include the Benaroya steps, the 1910 Cobb Building, and the awesome Art Deco skyscraper called the Seattle Tower.

Length:	**2.5 miles**
Walking Time:	1 hour 15 minutes
Steps Down:	385
Steps Up:	455
Kid-Friendly:	This stairway walk is mostly about steps and architecture, and thus is probably less interesting for kids.
Cafes/Pubs:	Yes, all kinds, all over! Aside from Pike Place Market and the area around it, the Colman Building has two pubs, Fado and the Owl N' Thistle. Midway through, you'll pass Fonté Coffee Roaster's cafe and wine bar between Harbor Steps and the Main Street stairs. At the start/end of the route, the Central Library has a nice cafe.

Getting There: Various local King County Metro Transit and Community Transit routes from places like Everett, Lynnwood, Issaquah, and Mercer Island stop at 4th and Cherry, near the first stairway at City Hall. Check

Looking back down the City Hall stairs

their websites at http://tripplanner.kingcounty.gov or www.commtrans.org. If you're driving, we recommend parking beneath Seattle's Central Library at 1000 4th Avenue. The entrance is off Spring Street, between 4th and 5th avenues. Parking is available throughout the week; weekend rates are very reasonable. At the Central Library web page (www.spl.org/locations/central -library), click on "Plan a Visit" and "Getting There & Parking" for current times and rates.

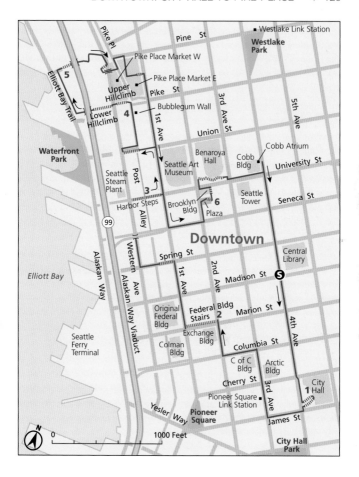

City Hall (65 steps up): From either the Central Library parking garage or the 4th and Cherry bus stop, head south along the east side of 4th Avenue. At the southeast corner with Cherry Street, you'll notice a tall glass-and-steel atrium with colored glass discs suspended inside; behind it stands City Hall. The "new" City Hall building opened in 2005. Features like abundant glass and a "green" rooftop **WWW** are meant to symbolize the open governance and environmental values on which Seattle prides itself.

Your stairway destination lies ahead, just beyond the open plaza on your left. These City Hall stairs (1) carry you all the way into the building, near the Council Chambers, though our official route stops just short of that. The staircase curves and narrows slightly toward the top, creating an inviting yet majestically sweeping effect. On the left a "seasonal" stream flows in a sculpted channel. It originates in a pool in front of the Seattle Municipal Tower one block east, disappears down a drain there, then reappears inside City Hall and flows outside here.

Walk up the 65 stairs, stopping at the base of the final flight leading into the building. On the left is an outside mezzanine area with tables and chairs, overlooking the street-level plaza you passed by earlier. To your right, a passageway leads to the side of the building, providing your exit.

Before leaving, consider taking the stairs up to the entrance of the open, soaring lobby (accessible weekdays). There are more stairs inside, and a favorite feature of ours is the *Blue Glass Passage* sculpture by James Carpenter. It's a deep blue functional glass walkway that extends high across the west lobby, connecting the mayor's offices to the Council Chambers. From up there looking out, you'll get great views of Puget Sound and the Olympics.

Blue Glass Passage is one of roughly 380 permanently sited works of public art that have been placed around the city under the 1973 "1 Percent for Art" ordinance, setting aside 1 percent of all city capital project monies for a public art fund. We'll point out several more "1 Percent for Art" installations along the way.

Arctic Building to the Federal Building Stairs (95 steps down, 5 steps up): At the base of that final flight of stairs up to the doors of City Hall, turn right, following the sidewalk around the corner of the building. It takes you down 10 steps to James Street; then turn right. After crossing 4th Avenue, walk downhill along James for one block. As you go, look ahead for the "sinking ship" parking garage, affectionately considered one of the ugliest buildings in Seattle. It's a triangular structure built against the grade so cars can enter directly from the street at all four levels. As a result, the "prow" on the downhill side pitches way up, like it's slipping under.

Turn right onto 3rd Avenue, keeping to the east side of the street. As you approach Cherry Street, look for the Arctic Building (1916) at the northeast corner. Listed on the National Register of Historic Places, this Seattle Landmark once housed the Arctic Club, a group of 1500 of the region's wealthiest businessmen and professionals. Today it's the Arctic Club Hotel, owned by DoubleTree.

Don't miss the twenty-seven terra-cotta walrus heads, complete with huge tusks, that wrap around the third-floor exterior. **WWW** The creamy white tusks are highlighted by a salmon-colored background, which contrasts beautifully with submarine-blue inset stripes. The Arctic Building is considered groundbreaking in its liberal use of pigmented terra-cotta facing, an innovation that added lightness and color to a drab city environment.

Continue along 3rd Avenue one block to Columbia Street. Cross over, then turn left to walk down the north side of Columbia. This immediately positions you for a good view of the building across the street, signed "PACIFIC NORTHWEST TITLE COMPANY." Built in 1924 to house the Seattle Chamber of Commerce, its facade resembles that of a twelfth-century Italian Romanesque church. On either side of the entrance there's a frieze representing both native Puget-Salish and modern industries. Running high along the top gable are sculpted sandstone depictions of native animals in Washington State. This old temple to commerce is a Seattle Landmark. **WWW**

From here walk down to 2nd Avenue, cross over, and then head right, continuing along the sidewalk on the west side of 2nd. The last building before you cross Marion Street is the Exchange Building (1930), another Seattle Landmark. In a case of bad timing, it was built to house the regional commodity and stock exchanges just as the stock market crashed, so it was converted to general office use as soon as it opened. It was the last major construction in Downtown Seattle for the next twenty years.

The detailed decoration inside the lobby references some of the state's agricultural products, such as wheat sheaves, grapes, and tulips. On the outside, the entryway arch is an explosion of Art Deco detail, with brass window-surrounds that glow exuberantly on sunny mornings.

From here, cross over Marion Street. Just after you cross, look for the hatch-cover (manhole cover) in the sidewalk. It's one example of the hatch-cover art, supported by 1 Percent for Art funds, that's visible all over Downtown. Some covers, like this one, have street maps stamped into the metal, with a silvery steel button marking the "you are here" location. Others feature Tlingit-style whale art or stylized faces staring up from the depths. So far, six different artists have been commissioned to contribute designs. **WWW**

Step ahead on the sidewalk a few feet toward a lonely stone arch. It's the former entryway of the Burke Building (1895), one of three buildings demolished to make way for the Henry M. Jackson Federal Building (1974), which now fills the block. Another ornate decoration from the old Burke Building now sits atop a wall just around the corner, on Marion.

From the Burke arch, take five steps up to a small plaza and then start down the 85 steps next to the Federal Building (2), which cascade in a series of terraces between the building and Marion Street. **WWW** Some parts of this stairway were salvaged from the original buildings, including the sandstone frieze with the words "BURKE BUILDING" at the first landing. **WWW** Early photos show this fragment at the top of the Burke Building six floors up, directly over the entry arch.

To the Spring Street Stairs and Harbor Steps (32 steps down, 107 steps up): At the bottom of the Federal Building steps, you can look directly across 1st Avenue to see the original Federal Building. It was built in 1933 on the site where the Great Fire of 1889 began. The two cast-bronze urns standing tall on either side of the entrance were originally located on the University of Washington campus, as part of the 1909 Exposition.

Now turn your glance to the left, across Marion Street, where you'll see the Colman Building (there's a Starbucks in the corner). It was built immediately after the Great Fire of 1889 by engineer James M. Colman and is a Seattle Landmark, as well as on the National Register of Historic Places. Intriguingly, there's a boat buried under it. Colman bought the ship *Winsome* after it wrecked on Whidbey Island, had it towed to Seattle, filled it with soil, then left it under the foundation as fill.

James M. Colman plays an important role in Seattle in other ways; in 1882 he built the Colman Dock, which is today's Seattle Ferry Terminal, and his family donated large parts of Colman Park in Mount Baker in his name (see walk 20, "Mount Baker"). Today the Colman Building houses several businesses, including two pubs, Fado and the Owl N' Thistle.

Head right on 1st. Cross Madison Street at the next block, and then cross Spring Street. At this point you should be on the northeast corner of 1st Avenue and Spring. Turn to cross 1st and then continue along the north side of Spring to the stairs immediately ahead. Hint: Follow the duck tracks!

The Spring street stairs bottom out just as you cross Post Alley, on the right, which you'll see a couple of times again. For now, continue on and turn right at the next major street, Western Avenue. Head north on Western past Seneca Street. Just as you approach University Street, look ahead to the left for a view of the stacks of the Seattle Steam company. This plant burns natural gas and wood to create high-pressure steam, which is piped beneath Downtown streets all the way up to First Hill. The steam is used to heat almost 200 buildings; sterilize medical equipment; control the humidity inside the Seattle Art Museum; and as part of the production process for artisan products like Beecher's cheese and Pike beers.

At University Street turn right to start up the Harbor Steps (3). **WWW** Midway up, Post Alley crosses the steps from either side. At the top of Harbor Steps, you'll be right across from the Seattle Art Museum and its iconic *Hammering Man* sculpture, another 1 Percent for Art piece.

Harbor Steps is a privately held, publicly accessible park built by the Harbor Properties development company. It was started by the prominent Bullitt family, who came to Seattle in 1889 and made a fortune in timber, real estate, and eventually broadcasting, as founders of KING-TV. Stimson Bullitt promoted this mixed-income development, centered around a grand stairway that provides one of the few attractive links between Downtown and the Waterfront.

To the Union Street Stairs and Pike Place Hillclimb, via Bubblegum Wall (243 steps down): At the top of the Harbor Steps, turn left to walk up 1st Avenue. You'll pass Fonté Coffee Roaster's cafe and wine bar halfway down the block. Then, turn left onto Union Street. Just past the entrance to the Four Seasons Hotel, the street ends at the top of a staircase, then starts up again a few yards directly below, with 103 stairs bridging the gap. At the head of these stairs you'll get a very nice view across Elliott Bay to Duwamish Head, the northern tip of West Seattle.

When you reach the bottom of the stairs, make a U-turn to walk back up the Union street-end toward the Post Alley entrance on the left. On the right is a concrete wall with a jagged steel sculpture running around the top. The sculpture, *Seattle Garden* by Anne Sperry, was commissioned with 1 Percent for Art funds. It provides both art and security for the Seattle City Light substation behind the wall.

Turn left to walk under the "POST ALLEY" sign and continue up the brick and cobblestone lane. Where the Pike Place Market arches across the alleyway, the wall on the right is covered up to a height of 9 or 10 feet with chewing gum of various colors and conformations—names, symbols, animals, hearts, faces. You've reached the famous Bubblegum Wall of Post Alley (4)! **WWW**

Keep walking past the wall until the alley dead-ends; here it's possible to turn right and walk up the cobblestone ramp to the street level of Pike Place, but instead turn left, through a passage that leads to the upper Pike Place Hillclimb staircase. The 73 upper stairs take you from Post Alley down to Western Avenue, where you'll cross and continue down the Lower Hillclimb stairs.

As you switchback down the Upper Hillclimb staircase, look around for the unusual lighting fixtures: seven diminutive cast-aluminum human figures, each 30 inches tall, holding small light globes aloft. One walks upside-down on the ceiling; others stroll up and down the vertical walls; another walks along a handrail. **WWW** One is just stepping out of a small fabricated aluminum door high up a wall, maybe the portal they all emerged from. Actually, these figures came from the fertile mind of artist Dan Webb, with help from a 1 Percent for Art grant made as part of a 2010 stairway renovation here.

At the bottom of the staircase, cross Western Avenue to continue down the 67 stairs of the Lower Hillclimb.

The Switchback Stairs Back to Pike Place (171 steps up): At the bottom of the lower Hillclimb stairs, continue straight until you reach the Elliott Bay Trail, a bicycle/pedestrian path that runs parallel with Alaskan Way. A quick side trip here across Alaskan Way takes you to Waterfront Park, a great place for a waterside stroll. It's just south of the Seattle Aquarium. To continue with the route, turn right onto the Elliott Bay Trail. Walk past a parking lot on your right, followed by a small commercial building, where you'll see a street sign for Pine Street. Turn right onto Pine.

Pine Street at this point is just a short street-end that leads to your next set of 89 upward steps. These are older construction than any other steps on this walk, with wooden handrails secured to 1920s-vintage recycled electric streetcar rails. At the top, cross a driveway to reach a sidewalk that takes you up to Western Avenue.

At the street turn right. Follow the sidewalk, watching for the staircase sitting back from the street, on the right (5). Its 60 stairs lead to the overhead walkway across Western Avenue, and into the main level of Pike Place. The official route doesn't include much of Pike Place, but this could be an opportunity for a side trip. Double doors at the end of the walkway take you into the market. To continue on the main route, wade ahead through the crowd, aiming very slightly left, and you'll reach another double door leading to the outside.

Once you're outside on cobblestoned Pike Place, head left to where it intersects Pine Street. Before you turn right to head up Pine, check out Beecher's Cheese on the corner across the way. It has a huge plate-glass viewing window, where you might be able to watch the early stages of cheese production taking place inside huge vats. Free samples can be had inside as well.

Walk a few steps up Pine and then turn right into yet another section of Post Alley. On your right, you're walking alongside a triangular-shaped building toward the pointed end. There, just before you merge back onto Pike Place, turn left to go into the east section of Pike Place Market. Head straight to the back, and you'll see a set of 22 lovely fir stairs heading up. **WWW** At the top, head outside the building to 1st Avenue and turn right.

Architectural Treasures, and Stairs Hidden in Plain Sight (107 steps up, 15 steps down): Walk south along 1st Avenue, next to the east-side market shops, crossing cobblestoned Pike Street. Continue on 1st for one block, to Union Avenue. At Union, cross over to the eastern side of 1st Avenue, and continue along 1st next to the Seattle Art Museum. Check out the *Hammering Man* kinetic sculpture just before you cross University Street. **WWW** At the next block turn left up Seneca Street, cross 2nd Avenue, and then turn left to walk north along the east side of 2nd. Before mid-block on your right you'll see a plaza set back from the street (6). Head up a couple of stairs and onto the plaza.

Here you can view an enigmatic, gleaming steel sculpture, *New Archetypes*. It looks as if several Tuscan columns were sliced-and-diced and then dropped from the sky. **WWW** Some stuck together, more or less, but others scattered when they hit. Two French artists, Patrick and Anne Poirier, created the work for this site in 1990. It includes their trademark, sitting in a reflecting pool: a huge chrome arrow that looks like it's been hurled from the sky, driven deep into a boulder. **WWW** Behind the pool are the bases of two well-hidden opposing stairways. Walk around to either side and head up 36 steps to a small mezzanine overlooking the street-level plaza.

Looking up the Benaroya stairs to Seattle Tower

From the mezzanine you can crane directly upwards for a close-up view of the outward-bulging side of the old WaMu (Washington Mutual) building. Today it's often referred to as "The 1201 Third Avenue Building," or "The Sparkplug". **WWW** At 772 feet this building is second in height only to the Columbia Tower (932 feet). It's in the Postmodern style, a disparate blend of architectural styles from far-flung eras. After the building went up in 1988, it received positive critical notice for successfully melding classical and modernist elements into a graceful, unified form.

The builders partially preserved one of the existing buildings on the site, the Brooklyn Building (1890), a Seattle Landmark. This Romanesque Revival structure, on the north side of the mezzanine **WWW**, is one of the few buildings still standing that was erected right after the Great Fire. Walk toward the Brooklyn Building to find the hidden stairway to University Street.

Between the Brooklyn Building and the corner of the 1201 Third Avenue Building, you'll see a covered stairway leading down to the street. After a quick

15 steps you'll be at the bottom; turn left, to the corner of University Street and 2nd Avenue. Cross University, then head up a few stairs into a small plaza next to Benaroya Hall. This is the Garden of Remembrance, a half-acre park dedicated to the memory of Washington's war dead, from 1941 forward. Amid trees and reflecting pools, there's a black granite wall facing west, with 8000 names etched into its shiny surface.

Head up the 71 stairs that curve up between the south side of Benaroya Hall and University Street. As you go up, look ahead through the trees lining the sidewalk for a view of our next Art Deco architectural gem. It's on the other side of University, on the far side of 3rd up ahead. When you reach the top of the Benaroya stairs, first cross 3rd and then turn right across University. This puts you at the southeast corner of the intersection, right next to the Seattle Tower.

Here sits Seattle's first Art Deco building, built in 1928 as a celebration of the age of technology. The Seattle Tower is on the National Register of Historic Places and is a Seattle Landmark. The 33 shades of brick on its face get progressively lighter toward the top **WWW**, which is said to reflect the region's mountains and rock formations while giving an air of lightness to this twenty-seven-story, ziggurat-like building. If you're here during the weekday, we recommend a look inside the ornate lobby.

From here, head east on University to the next block, watching for the Cobb Building across the street at the corner of 4th. The Cobb, built in 1910 as a dedicated medical building (an innovation at the time), has recently been repurposed as a luxury apartment building. It boasts a green LEED rating, in part thanks to steam heating from the Seattle Steam plant down the hill.

The Beaux-Arts style combines classical proportion with elaborate ornamentation; as an exemplar of this style, the Cobb has been put on the National Register of Historic Places. The proportions are delineated by the elaborate cream-colored terra-cotta facing on the tall first floor and the top two floors; brick is used in-between. There's a lot of fancy ornamentation, especially around the top: our favorite is the terra-cotta Indian heads, set into paired cartouches beneath elaborate window arches. **WWW** You can detour up 4th Avenue a few steps to reach the exterior atrium facing the street. There you can see one of these surprisingly large heads up close.

To close the loop and end your walk, start south on 4th Avenue, passing alongside the historic Fairmont Olympic Hotel, located diagonally across from the Cobb, on the site of the first University of Washington building. After just two blocks, you'll find yourself back at the Central Library, near your parking spot or bus stop.

16 Fauntleroy and Morgan Junction

On this walk there's just one "up" stairway, with only 69 steps. On the other hand, you'll visit the second-longest set of stairs in Seattle, the Thistle stairs in Fauntleroy. This stairway has 367 steps, so this walk does confer some bragging rights, even if you're only going down. The Howe stairway on Capitol Hill is the longest, with 388 steps, but the Thistle stairs are a close rival, in terms of both steps and views.

This walk is a wide-ranging exploration of both the Fauntleroy and Morgan Junction neighborhoods. At the bottom of the Thistle stairs you'll head toward little-known Solstice Park, with its giant stone-and-earthworks astrolabe. Then you'll cross under the tall second-growth trees of Lincoln Park to a bluff overlooking the edge of Puget Sound. All of this happens in the core of Fauntleroy neighborhood.

From the base of the bluff stairs you'll head north and inland, to "discover" a set of hidden stairs on the way to Morgan Junction. You can take a break at one of the cafes and pubs in this small but active commercial district before making a beeline south on California Avenue, to your starting place.

Length:	**3.5 miles**
Walking Time:	1 hour 45 minutes
Steps Down:	495
Steps Up:	69
Kid-Friendly:	Walk 17, "Solstice Park," is in this same general area but is shorter and offers more reliable access to restrooms, parks, and play areas.
Cafes/Pubs:	You'll find Caffe Ladro at the start, and a variety of eateries at the north end of the route, at Morgan Junction. If you love microbrews, you can't do much better than Beveridge Place Pub at the junction; it has twenty-two handles on rotation as well as wine, cider, and mead (bring your own food or order from a nearby eatery).

Getting There: Metro Transit Route 22 stops near the beginning, at California SW and SW Myrtle Street. If you're driving, park near Caffe Ladro, 7011 California Avenue SW, just north of SW Myrtle.

To the Thistle Stairs (367 steps down): From the junction of SW Myrtle Street and California Avenue SW, walk south along the west side of California for one block, past SW Othello Street and 44th Avenue SW. These two streets follow each other in quick succession from the right. Just beyond 44th Avenue SW, you pass a modernistic, cedar-sided home. Turn right up an unmarked lane, with the home's garage just to your right. The lane quickly veers to the left uphill, then straightens, taking you into an interesting neighborhood with a quieter ambience than you'll find along California Avenue.

You'll be strolling down this unnamed lane or alley, paralleling California Avenue, for the next quarter mile. Along the way you'll pass three unsigned streets coming in from the left side, with counterpart walkways and stairs to the right. After the first one there's a real intersection, where the street does go through left to right. This is SW Austin, though there's no street sign nearby. Cross Austin, and about five houses along look for SW Ida Street coming in from the left (again, no street sign). On the right opposite Ida, there's another walkway/stairway, with a charming little bench and viewpoint at the top. It has a good view of Blake Island looking west over the treetops of Lincoln Park, which you'll be walking through later.

Continue south to unsigned SW Holden Street, coming in from the left. Here there's yet another little stairway on the right, heading down between two tall laurel hedges. One block later, turn left onto SW Portland Street (after you turn away, the lane continues ahead for a half block before finally ending at a ravine).

Walk one block east on Portland, then turn right onto California Avenue SW, heading south. After four blocks on California, turn right onto SW Southern Street. Then you'll take the first left at Northrop Place SW, but before you do that, check out the colorful mosaic art along a driveway just a couple of houses past Northrop, on the right. **WWW**

Walk south for one block on Northrop until it ends at SW Thistle Street. Here you'll find the head of the Thistle stairs (1) and probably some friendly neighborhood types using the stairs to exercise themselves and/or their dogs. Head down the first flight, which is briefly interrupted at its junction with 44th Avenue SW. The stairs end at 46th Avenue SW. Turn right onto 46th, heading north.

To Solstice Park: As you walk north on 46th Avenue toward Solstice Park, you'll be paralleling Fauntleroy Way SW, just below you to the west. Your higher route here is less trafficked than Fauntleroy, and more scenic, but with a jog or two to negotiate.

At its intersection with SW Rose Street, 46th Avenue SW forks almost imperceptibly to the left. Stay to the left side; the right fork becomes SW Hemlock Way. Follow 46th Avenue to its T junction with SW Monroe Street.

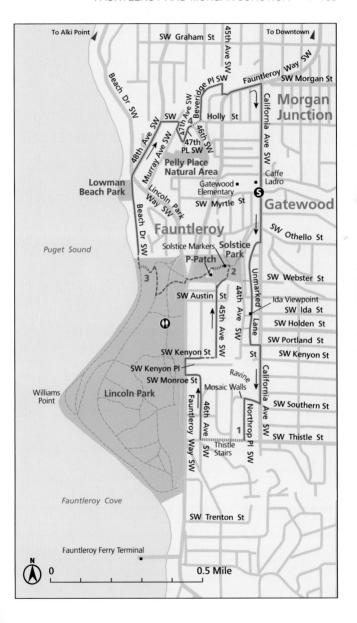

Looking down the Thistle stairs—367 to go!

Head downhill on Monroe and then turn right onto Fauntleroy, going north. Pass SW Kenyon Place, then turn right onto SW Kenyon Street. One block up on Kenyon Street you'll encounter 46th Avenue again, running off to the left. Continue straight ahead up a steep sidewalk/path to the next block up. Turn left here, onto SW 45th Avenue, and walk north on SW 45th several blocks toward Solstice Park.

One block past SW Austin Street, the street forks. Follow the right fork, which becomes a broad, gravel path as it leads up the hill into the park. Walk to the top of Solstice Park (2), where you can view the solar-tracking earthworks and the Olympics across the Sound to the west.

See walk 17 for more highlights of Solstice Park and a shorter route from the same starting point.

To Lincoln Park Bluff Stairs and North Beach Trail (128 steps down): From Solstice Park's overview, turn down the hill, following a switchbacking timber stairway through the P-Patch neighborhood garden (28 timber steps). Head past the southeast corner of the tennis courts (on your right) to Fauntleroy Way SW. Take both lighted crosswalks, first across Fauntleroy and then across 47th Avenue SW, so that you end up walking south on Fauntleroy. Just a few feet beyond the second crosswalk, take the pedestrian entrance to the right, up a few stairs, into Lincoln Park.

Walk across the park, angling left from Fauntleroy Way. You'll pass a picnic area, a play area, and a restroom to your left on the way to a path and wooden fence at the edge of the bluff, overlooking Puget Sound. Take the path right, walking along the bluff to the northern edge of the park. (An alternate route has you turning left here.) WWW There, just past a giant madrona tree, you'll see a timber archway on the left, lettered "N. BEACH TRAIL," marking the top of the Bluff stairs (3). This is a lovely mixed stairway/path switching back and forth down the side of the bluff, dropping about 130 feet to the beach via 100 timber steps. WWW

At the bottom of the North Beach Trail, look left toward Colman Pool and Williams Point; around the point are Fauntleroy Cove and the ferry dock. Straight across the water is Blake Island. Turn right onto the wide gravel beachside path, and head north. WWW

Once you exit Lincoln Park, the path broadens into a vehicle/pedestrian lane. You'll spend the next few minutes walking through residential areas southwest of Morgan Junction. The houses along the beach are varied and interesting, while the slope on the right side is steep and heavily wooded in most places, and landslide-prone. The lane becomes a full-fledged street as you come to Lowman Beach Park.

Lowman Beach Park to the Hidden Beveridge Stairs (69 steps up): Take the sidewalk running between the street and the park. At the northern border of the park, just past the tennis courts, you'll see a somewhat complicated intersection with stop signs. Lincoln Park Way runs uphill sharply to your right, while 48th Avenue SW runs uphill straight inland.

Carefully cross Lincoln Park Way toward the east side of 48th Avenue SW. As you head uphill on 48th you'll pass a dozen or so houses on your right, before arriving at SW Holly Street. Turn right onto Holly.

After three houses on the right, Holly turns sharply right and becomes Murray Avenue SW. Continue on Murray a couple of dozen feet, then veer to your left away from Murray onto 47th Avenue SW. In another few dozen feet, just before 47th Avenue SW dead-ends, again turn sharply left onto 47th Place SW.

The hidden Beveridge stairs

Continue uphill on 47th Place SW. When the street veers uphill and to the right (becoming 46th Avenue SW), keep walking straight ahead, up what appears to be a driveway; there is often a car parked here. Skirt this driveway along its left border, and you'll quickly discover a discreet stairway tucked in back: the Beveridge stairs (4).

Believe it or not, these 69 steps are the most you'll climb on this walk! Turn left at the top, following Beveridge Place SW, as it gradually curves to the right before finally making a 90-degree right turn to become 45th Avenue SW. At this point you'll be able to see busy Fauntleroy Way straight ahead. At Fauntleroy, turn left, walking along the sidewalk toward Morgan Junction, at the intersection of Fauntleroy and California Avenue SW. There are various cafe/pub possibilities here. To return to the start, walk south on California Avenue SW.

17 Solstice Park

If you're looking for a stairway walk that's short, sweet, and memorable, here's the ticket. This 45-minute route in the Fauntleroy neighborhood of West Seattle, just over a mile long, offers a couple of brief stairways, great views of Lincoln Park and Puget Sound, and possibilities for a leisurely picnic on a sunny day.

The walk centers on fascinating Solstice Park, with its massive stone-and-earthworks astrolabe—an instrument for calculating the position of stars and other celestial bodies. It tops an artificial hill created here to keep a slide zone tamped into place.

The astrolabe is formed from three wide, stone-lined trenches that intersect each other through a head-high, semicircular berm. By facing Puget Sound and

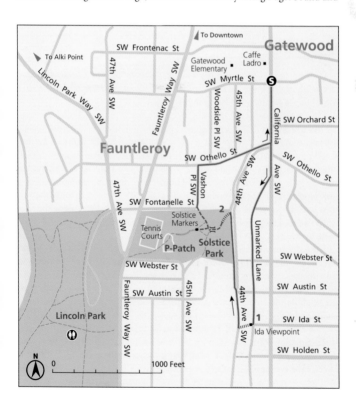

lining up each trench with a corresponding stone marker beyond the berm, you can see where on the horizon the sun will set on a given solstice day.

Doug Beyerlein, who maintains a comprehensive map of major Seattle stairways (WWW), grew up on nearby Gatewood Hill. As a kid, he and his friends would build forts right here, in what they considered "wild forest." Decades later, it's a neighborhood gem with a completely different character. The "wild forest" has been domesticated, but West Seattle's version of Stonehenge still imparts a sense of awe and wonder.

Length:	**1 mile**
Walking Time:	45 minutes
Steps Down:	70
Kid-Friendly:	Kids will love the astrolabe and the P-Patch garden at Solstice Park.
Cafes/Pubs:	Caffe Ladro is near the starting/ending place, and nearby Morgan Junction offers several places where you can get food and drink.

Getting There: Metro Transit Route 22 stops at California Avenue SW and SW Myrtle, near the start. If you come by car, park near Caffe Ladro, at 7011 California Avenue SW, just north of SW Myrtle.

To the Ida Stairs (24 steps down): From the junction of California Avenue SW and SW Myrtle Street, head south on the west side of California Avenue. You'll pass SW Othello Street and then 44th Avenue SW within steps of each other, as they merge with California Avenue from your right. After 44th Avenue and just past a modernist cedar-sided home, turn right up an unmarked lane, passing the home's garage on the right. The lane quickly veers to the left uphill, then straightens. There are many interesting homes to gawk at along the way, and it's a quieter experience than California Avenue, which closely parallels your route for the next quarter mile or so.

Continue toward the first complete left/right street intersection (SW Austin Street). On the way there, you'll pass a tempting little stairway between tall laurel hedges, where an unmarked SW Webster Street ends. Five houses down on the right, where SW Ida Street comes in from the left (1), somebody from the neighborhood has placed a sweet little bench, with a wonderful view of the Sound and Blake Island, visible over the tops of the trees in Lincoln Park. (WWW) From the bench, head down a combined stairway/walkway (24 steps).

To Solstice Park (46 steps down): At the bottom of the Ida stairs, turn right onto 44th Avenue SW, reversing your direction to the north. Back at Austin Street, 44th Avenue SW divides into two lanes. Walk up the southbound lane on your left. At this point, it's separated from the northbound, upslope portion of

Descending into Solstice Park

44th Avenue by a retaining wall, partly constructed by old trolley rails and slabs. There's no sidewalk here, so keep an eye out for any cars heading your way.

Just before your lane of 44th veers uphill and to the right, look for the top of a stairway on the left (2). Here, 46 timber stairs wind gracefully down into Solstice Park.

WHAT'S A P-PATCH?

The "P" in P-Patch stands for the Picardo family, who sold their farmland to the city in the 1970s as the first Seattle community garden. The P-Patch program involves more than seventy community gardens today, with a mix of city and other ownership. According to the Seattle Department of Neighborhoods, in 2009 the various P-Patches around the city gave more than 13 tons of fresh food to people in need. The Lincoln Park Annex P-Patch was champion donor that year, producing more than six tons per acre. For more info on P-Patch Community Gardens, go to www.cityofseattle.net/neighborhoods/ppatch.

At the base of the stairs just beyond a little footbridge, note the gravel pathway leading to the right and north out of the park; you'll use it later.

To Solstice Park and Back: Once down the stairs, you'll have panoramic views of the Sound and the Olympic Mountains. Here too you can explore the solstice sunset markers, aligning the trenches and stone markers to visualize the various solstice sunset points. The hill-sized berm beneath your feet was created in the 1980s to stabilize the base of a slide zone behind you; the trenches and solstice markers were added in 2002.

For more background on Solstice Park, check out the Seattle Parks website, www.cityofseattle.net/parks/proparks/projects/lincolnannex.htm.

For a brief side trip, venture down the path and another 28 timber steps toward the P-Patch garden. You can also cross Fauntleroy Avenue below the tennis courts to explore Lincoln Park (see walk 16, "Fauntleroy and Morgan Junction," for adventures into Lincoln Park and beyond).

Back to the Beginning: Loop back to your starting place using the path to the park's north exit (mentioned above). Step straight ahead onto Vashon Place SW. (SW Fontanelle Street runs downhill at this juncture. Here, you can see the slide zone upheaval, in both the street and sidewalk.) Continue north on Vashon Place SW until it ends at SW Othello Street.

Turn right onto Othello and walk up the hill toward California Avenue. The apartment building on the left, just before the Unitarian Universalist church at the corner, houses artists' studios. It's open to visitors during the West Seattle Art Walk (www.westseattleartwalk.blogspot.com), held monthly on every second Thursday. If you look through the lobby window, you may see some of the resident artists' work on display.

At California and Othello, you're near your starting point. A coffee and pastry at Caffe Ladro, to the left on California, might be a nice way to cap off your urban hike!

18 Alki from Above

Alki Beach is a year-round magnet for tourists, and a very popular summertime destination for Seattleites too. Take a summer drive around the peninsula, and your eyes tend to be drawn outward—to the sand, the water, and the festive folks strolling the boardwalk.

The ferry, heading from Downtown past Alki Point, provides a very different view. From this perspective a 300-foot bluff—Duwamish Head—dominates and defines Alki. If you're a neighborhood explorer and stairway walker, this view will start you thinking about the possibilities for exploration. Is there a route from the top of the bluff to the beach below—maybe a stairway or two with a view? You'll find out on this walk, which starts in the North Admiral neighborhood at the top of the peninsula, advances to the bluff's edge, then plunges down steep lanes and scenic stairways toward the beach. Along the way you'll get intimate views of a proudly independent neighborhood, clinging tenaciously to the hillside.

In summertime, down at the beach it's crowded and colorful, a great place to watch people having fun on the sand with families and friends. The off-season vibe is quieter, more conducive to appreciating gorgeous views across

Stairs down to Schmitz Preserve Park from SW Admiral Way

the Sound all the way to the Olympics. In any season you can sample from one of many cafes and food joints up and down Alki Way before heading back up the bluff's back streets and stairs to Schmitz Preserve Park. Along with Seward Park next to Lake Washington, Schmitz Preserve Park is one of just two places in Seattle where you can walk among old-growth trees, and it's one of the treasures of the neighborhood.

Length:	**3.4 miles**
Walking Time:	2 hours and 20 minutes
Steps Down:	374
Steps Up:	73
Kid-Friendly:	This walk will be long for most kids under age six or seven, and the final leg in Schmitz Preserve Park gets steep. Even elementary-age kids will need supervision along some streets and street crossings. On the other hand, the turnaround point at Alki Beach can be great for kids, so one alternative is to start your walk at Alki Beach, exploring the 53rd Avenue and Bonair Street stairs from there (see map).
Cafes/Pubs:	You'll find numerous spots for a break or a meal along Alki Beach.

Getting There: There's plenty of parking along SW Spokane Street at 49th Avenue SW, near Schmitz Park Elementary. Pay attention to the signs, though, as some stretches are restricted. If you're taking the bus, King County Metro RapidRide C runs from Downtown to Alaska Junction; from there, take MT 50 or MT 128, West Seattle routes that stop at the corner of California Ave SW and SW Spokane Street, near where this walk begins.

Schmitz Preserve Park can be muddy and soggy after it rains, so bring water-resistant boots if you have any doubts about trail conditions there.

North Admiral to College Street Ravine: On your way through the North Admiral neighborhood, you'll encounter a sequence of block-to-block turns: From SW Spokane Street, head north on 49th Avenue SW, then turn left onto SW Hanford Street. Turn right at the next street, 50th Avenue SW, and one block later turn left onto SW Stevens Street. At the next block turn right onto Garlough Avenue SW, heading north for one block until you reach SW Admiral Way. This will be the first of two crossings of busy Admiral Way. Sight lines are good, but there's no crosswalk and traffic moves fast, so double-check that it's clear and move with dispatch! Garlough Avenue continues as a small lane on the other side of Admiral, running in the same northerly direction, but displaced 10 yards or so to the east. When Garlough ends in a T intersection with SW Waite Street, turn left onto Waite.

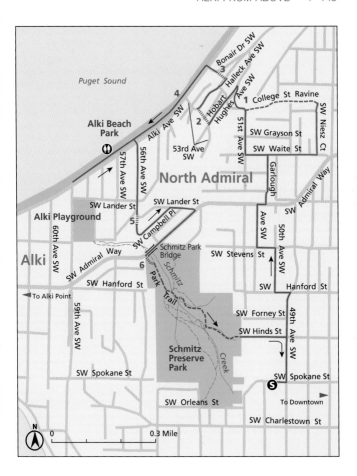

On the right side of Waite, before you reach the next corner, look for a house peeking out from a dense front garden, spotted all over with colorful geometric designs and sculptures. You may see the Chippewa flag flying at the corner of the house. The owners' Native American heritage provides the inspiration for these abstract and eye-pleasing decorations. The tasteful, fascinating results are everywhere—on the chimney, eaves, fences, and front gate. **WWW**

From SW Waite, turn right onto 51st Avenue SW. The second house on the left is a low-slung, angular Midcentury-style home, one of our favorites.

At SW Grayson Street you might want to take a quick detour to another "dream home" at the street-end, where you'll get your first views of the Sound.

Back on 51st, continue walking north as the street heads more steeply downhill. There are some cool homes along here too, both Midcentury and newly constructed. Eventually, the road takes a sharp turn to the left to become SW College Street. At the outside of the turn is a trail (1) entering what is locally known as the College Street Ravine, a quiet, heavily forested section of the Duwamish Head Greenbelt. If the path is dry and you're feeling intrepid, consider a quick detour here (see "Option: College Street Ravine Loop"), eight blocks round-trip. (WWW)

Option: College Street Ravine Loop

The North Admiral neighborhood is situated at the northern tip of the West Seattle peninsula, known as Duwamish Head. Duwamish Head looms about 300 feet high, terminating just before the water in a steep, forested bluff that runs from Harbor Island on the east all the way around the peninsula to Alki on the west. The Duwamish Head Greenbelt covers most of that bluff. College Street Ravine is a small inland incursion of the greenbelt at its southwest end.

Enter the ravine at the trailhead (1) next to the "DUWAMISH HEAD GREENBELT" sign. The trail covers the entire length of this short ravine, which is also the unused right-of-way for College Street. You'll probably see signs of plant restoration work taking place here, but be aware that you might need to walk around fallen branches or through somewhat overgrown sections of trail. Where the ravine comes to an end the trail makes a right turn, toward the street-end at SW Niesz Court. At the edge of the pavement, look for a box that's often stuffed with anonymous poetry written for passersby. After reading a poem or contributing your own, continue one block south on Niesz Court to SW Waite Street, and turn right. Follow Waite about four blocks back to 51st Avenue SW. Turn right on 51st to get back to where you started, at SW College Street. ♦

To the 53rd Avenue Stairs (186 steps down): Now you'll move down the bluff above Alki Beach, exploring some nooks and crannies along the way. At College Street the road turns down the side of Alki Bluff. As you make your way down the narrow lane, walk single-file (if in a group) and well over to one side, facing oncoming traffic. As the street turns sharply right, it narrows further, steepens, and becomes 52nd Avenue SW. The trees close in, forming a beautiful canopy over the street from both sides. Here, you begin your trek down the bluff in earnest!

You'll quickly arrive at an intersection where Hughes Avenue SW comes up to meet you from the left. Turn left onto Hughes and head south, passing SW College Street, which slopes steeply off to the right. After that, the road levels out.

As you proceed on Hughes, look ahead for a street sloping down from the left, marked by a "DEAD END" sign. This is 53rd Avenue SW. To your right, follow the sidewalk away from Hughes and between two houses, to your first stairway of the walk. WWW

STAIRWAY EVOLUTION IN SEATTLE

The City began recycling long before it became twenty-first-century routine! By 1941, wheeled electric buses had replaced the City's rail streetcar system. The City began removing the steel rails and the concrete slabs between them, filling the space with material to match the rest of the street.

The leftover rails and concrete slabs were ingeniously reused as stairways and retaining walls in many areas of town, at least up until about 1965. The slabs were stacked to form stairs or walls, while the old streetcar rails were used as upright posts to secure handrails and walls. WWW About 130 of the SDOT-owned stairways in the city were built with these surplus materials, as a thrifty if less durable alternative to the ornate reinforced cast-concrete stairways built in the early decades of the twentieth century. Check out walk 11, "Southwest Queen Anne," for beautiful examples of the older, "classic" style.

Today's SDOT stairways are intended to conform to the Americans with Disabilities Act (ADA). Refurbished stairways now have double handrails, and a usable width of 6 feet. WWW SDOT has recently experimented with adding a bicycle wheel "runnel" to an existing stairway at Admiral Way SW and SW Spokane Street, so bicyclists can push their bikes up the stairs. After getting positive response, SDOT decided to add this "bicycle portage" feature wherever stairways are part of the right-of-way in the City's Bicycle Master Plan.

The new design is being implemented as part of the $365 million "Bridging the Gap" levy, passed by Seattle voters in 2006. Through 2016, the initiative will address many of the city's transportation maintenance and improvement needs, including planned rehabilitation of forty to fifty stairways. SDOT targets stairways for upgrade based on safety, condition, number of users, and geographic distribution. It's also possible for neighborhoods to be "squeaky wheels" on behalf of their own stairways!

The 53rd Avenue stairs (2) are a good place to see the varieties of stairway construction and materials used over the years. The initial steps are much narrower than what gets built today. Also, notice the repurposed streetcar rails that serve as vertical supports for the wooden handrails. According to SDOT, this section of stairs was built in 1924, though some of its materials might be from a later refurbishment (see "Stairway Evolution in Seattle").

Halfway down, the stairs show evidence of more recent construction with different materials. The treads have steel "nosings" for durability, and the side rails are made of cylindrical steel pipe, riveted in place. The first flight empties onto the street-end at Hobart Avenue SW. Just across the street you'll find the second flight, a spanking-new stairway rebuilt in 2009 under the city's "Bridging the Gap" program.

To the Bonair Stairs (109 steps down): As soon as you get to the bottom of the second flight of 53rd Avenue stairs, turn right onto Halleck Avenue SW. The uphill stretch here gets a bit steeper as you approach SW College Street, which drops down from your right. But take heart: just past College Street, where your path jogs slightly left, look for a break in the railing on the left side of the street. That's the landing for your next stairway down: the Bonair Drive SW stairs (3).

Here at the top of the Bonair stairs you'll get the best views between November and March, when the trees are bare. You can see the beach, Alki Point, and all the way across the Sound. In the summer months the stairs seem to dive down into a leafy tunnel; in late summer, you might find ripe blackberries along the way.

The stairs end in a sidewalk, with an apartment complex on your left. On your right, Bonair Drive SW comes alongside as you march ahead toward Alki Avenue SW. The next section of the route is an out-and-back excursion along Alki Beach.

Alki Beach Walk: As you approach Alki Avenue SW, look for the marked crosswalk that will take you across the street. On the other side, turn left onto the Alki Trail (4). The "boardwalk" (actually a concrete sidewalk) is marked on its surface with a "walking man" symbol. As you head southwest toward Alki Point, it's safest to stay on the pedestrian walk, avoiding the separate bicycle lane.

In less than 10 minutes (0.4 mile), you'll come to a public restroom. Note this as a landmark, about one block south of where you'll head back up the bluff via the 56th Avenue stairs.

For now, continue south down the Alki Trail boardwalk toward the Old Bathhouse (also known as Alki Art Studio), along the busiest section of the beach. There are many items of interest along the way: a display about harbor seal pups, which sometimes sleep on the beach; various plaques and installations about the history and life of Alki, from its first people forward; and a kiosk with maps of walking routes and stairways you can explore further. South of the bathhouse there's a park and waterside promenade, with lots of shops and cafes

Alki overlook, atop Bonair stairs

across the street. In a plaza just south of the bathhouse stands a treasured West Seattle landmark, the miniature Statue of Liberty. **WWW**

To the Hidden 56th Stairs and Admiral Way (55 steps up): Once you're ready to head back, follow the Alki Trail the way you came. One block north of the restrooms, cross Alki Avenue and head up 56th Avenue SW. The return climb will be more gradual than your descent.

At the end of a long block, you'll reach an intersection with 55th Avenue SW approaching from the left, and SW Lander Street from the right. Keep walking up 56th, but move over to the left side of the street, on the sidewalk. The street starts to rise, and then curves left (becoming SW Lander Place). Just past the start of the curve, and just beyond SW Teig Place on the right, cautiously cross to the other side of 56th (visibility around the corner is limited).

Across 56th, look for the stairway heading up the hill (5). These stairs, built in 1928, have an enchanting setting. They're several feet back from the street, so in the leafiest depths of summer you probably won't see them at first. At the top you're deposited onto a narrow, curving sidewalk that's closely hugged by a couple of small houses, with nice front gardens. It's a cozy, quaint space that quickly opens out onto SW Campbell Place, which you follow as it curves sharply to the left.

Walk uphill on Campbell for a long block until it ends in a T with SW Lander, where you turn right. Continue uphill on SW Lander to busy SW Admiral Way, and turn right again, onto Admiral.

Schmitz Preserve Park, Bridge, and Stairs (79 steps down, 22 steps up): Once you're on SW Admiral Way, you'll be following a sidewalk slightly downhill. After one long block, look across to see SW Stevens Street coming down to join Admiral. Just to the right of Stevens, you'll see a sign marking the entrance to Schmitz Preserve Park, and to the right you'll see a bridge. Cross Admiral here, heading toward the park sign. Be very careful with this crossing. Visibility is good in both directions, but traffic is moving fast, so you'll need to move quickly across once it's clear.

Turn right, heading along the sidewalk toward the 175-foot-long Schmitz Park Bridge (6). This soaring concrete bridge was constructed in 1936 by the WPA for just $134,000. It incorporated a new concrete-box technology that made the bridge significantly lighter and less expensive to construct, so it could be built 60 percent longer than any similar bridge. It's a Seattle Landmark and listed in the National Register of Historic Places. Even some of the graffiti at the base of the bridge has received national attention!

This bridge crosses a deep ravine, with Schmitz Park Creek running far below, at the base of tall trees that extend well above your head next to the bridge. From the middle, a look over the side gives a hint of what you're about to enter,

SCHMITZ PRESERVE PARK

Individual trees in the Schmitz Preserve Park ravine were logged here and there, and a windstorm in 1992 took another 100 trees, but Schmitz Preserve Park and Seward Park are still the only two parks or greenspaces in Seattle that still consist primarily of old-growth forest. In the case of Schmitz Preserve Park, it's said that the steep ravine made logging difficult here, giving Ferdinand Schmitz a chance to acquire the land in pristine condition.

Schmitz was a German immigrant who became a prominent Seattle banker and realtor. In 1908, he became the City's parks commissioner, and that same year donated 30 acres of the ravine as a park, with the express purpose of saving some of the last old-growth forest in Seattle. Over the ensuing years up until 1958, the city added more land, so the park today covers 53 acres. It has a variety of paths leading up different arms of the ravine, and it's a delightful place to get lost. In springtime, skunk cabbage **WWW** blooms all over the wetlands alongside the creek and its various tributaries. In summer you'll see salmonberries, thimbleberries, and Indian plum proliferating alongside the trails. Except for the occasional barking dog or sounds of kids at play, Schmitz Preserve Park is mostly a hushed sanctuary, perfect for strolling, birding, or botanizing. **WWW**

including the broad path you'll soon be taking up the ravine. **WWW** Here, in one of Seattle's last remnants of old-growth forest (see "Schmitz Preserve Park"), you can imagine what it may have been like when Seattle's founders, the Denny party, landed on Alki in 1851.

Once you've crossed Schmitz Park Bridge, on the left you'll see a timber stairway switchbacking down to the base of the bridge. At the bottom of the 79 steps, check out the graffiti along the base of the bridge, then turn right, heading up the ravine on a wide path.

At first the ravine is relatively open; here you can look across to the other side, with the creek visible well below. As you walk along, the creek quickly rises to trail level; the ravine narrows, and the creek disappears behind thick undergrowth.

Graffiti art beneath Schmitz Park Bridge

Turn left down the first side trail and into a tunnel of salmonberry and willow. You soon reach the creek, and cross over on a set of sturdy and artfully placed stepping-stones.

Until 2003, the creek here was covered with a parking lot, of all things. Using funding from the Pro Parks Levy, the parks department opened up the creek and put away the parking lot, a nice twist on the Joni Mitchell song. Invasive plants were replaced by native ones and the stream banks were rebuilt. Right after you cross the creek, head up a set of 22 timber stairs, also installed as part of the daylighting project.

At the top of the stairs, turn sharply right, away from two other trails moving off to the left. You'll then cross a short bridge, after which the trail curves left and steepens. A bit farther along, you'll hear and see a tributary of Schmitz Park Creek below and to the right, just before you pass a side trail on the left.

From here you'll be heading steadily up and out of the ravine, to exit on its eastern side; just keep left at the next trail junction. (If you want to explore more of Schmitz Preserve Park—and there's plenty more to explore—take a right at this junction instead. That will give you access to the entire southwestern trail system, where you can check out other ravines and streams.)

This is where the trail becomes steepest, but take your time—it's a great place to dawdle. Eventually, the trail emerges from Schmitz Park onto SW Hinds Street. Continue past a gate up Hinds to the first cross street, 49th Avenue SW. Turn right onto 49th and walk down the block to SW Spokane Street and your starting place.

19 Longfellow Creek and Pigeon Point

Crossing Longfellow Creek at Salmon Bone Bridge

As you drive into West Seattle, the West Seattle Bridge abruptly curves to avoid a hill looming up from the left. That hill is Pigeon Point, the northern tip of Puget Ridge, which stretches more than 4 miles away to the south.

Along the length of Puget Ridge grows the largest forest in Seattle, preserved as the Duwamish Greenbelt. It forms a rampart that dominates the western view from I-5, dividing the biggest neighborhood district in Seattle from the rest of the city. There's even a moat running along the base: the channelized, industrialized Duwamish River. Several West Seattle neighborhoods run in a line north to south on the other side of this barricade: Pigeon Point, Delridge, High Point, and White Center.

On this short stairway walk you'll explore the Pigeon Point neighborhood, perched almost invisibly among the trees. Thousands of people zoom below it every day, and it's surrounded by industry on three sides, but Pigeon Point itself is a comfortable, neighborly enclave with a generous mix of home types and a variety of glancing views.

The walk starts below the western slope of Pigeon Point, on the Longfellow Creek Legacy Trail. This has become one of the most pleasant and scenic sections of this year-round creek. Thanks to careful design and restoration work, and lots of caring volunteers, salmon and other native fish swim here again. The Legacy Trail also features vivid public sculptures and you'll actually walk through one of them on your way across the creek (think Jonah and the whale, or in this case Jonah and the giant salmon).

After exploring this showcase section of restored Longfellow Creek, you'll take a long stairway up the western side of Puget Ridge, with views of the Delridge Valley behind. At the top you'll meander north through neighborhood streets and a few more stairs to the tip of Pigeon Point. Then you'll angle down the east side of the ridge on another long stairway. At the bottom, the route ends with a stroll under the busy West Seattle Bridge, close to the thrumming industry that encircles Pigeon Point. This is very much a walk of contrasts, and all the more fascinating because of it!

Length:	**1.8 miles**
Walking Time:	1 hour 30 minutes
Steps Down:	274
Steps Up:	314
Kid-Friendly:	Longfellow Creek and its sculptures will be a big hit with kids of exploring age, and there's a park/restroom at the Delridge Community Center. Both occur early in the walk, for easy diversion and/or turnaround if needed. For older kids there's an active new skate park at the community center, right next to the walk.
Cafes/Pubs:	Delridge Deli and Skylark Cafe are at the end of the route, and local favorite Luna Park Cafe is on nearby Avalon Street, next to the West Seattle Bridge.

Getting There: The nearest major cross streets are Delridge Way SW and SW Andover Street. If you're driving into West Seattle from the bridge, take the Delridge exit and turn right onto SW Andover heading west; take the next left onto 26th Avenue SW, then the first right onto SW Yancy Street. Park either in the lot on the south side, or streetside. Metro Transit Routes 120 and 125 stop at Delridge and Andover.

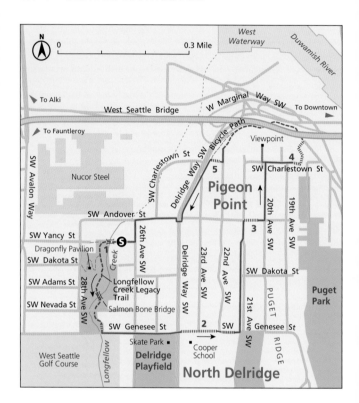

Longfellow Creek Legacy Trail and Stairs (35 steps up): If you're arriving by bus, from your stop at Delridge and Andover, just follow the above driving directions on foot, making your way to 26th and Yancy. From here, everybody's on the same page: walk west on Yancy toward the wooded area ahead.

Enter the Longfellow Creek Legacy Trail (1) using the footbridge over the creek, then turn left to follow the trail upstream. You'll quickly pass another footbridge on the left, but keep to the main trail.

Keep an eye on the right, where on a knoll above you might glimpse a giant dragonfly sculpture. This *Dragonfly Pavilion*, along with the Salmon Bone Bridge just ahead, was designed by Lorna Jordan as part of Seattle Public Utilities' Urban Creeks Legacy Program.

After the Salmon Bone Bridge you'll pass a stairway heading up to your left, just before a street overpass. Soon after, there's a short observation bridge heading off to your right, dead-ending on the opposite side of the creek. (WWW) Here the main path begins a slow S curve before reaching the base of a stairway that will take you up from the creek to SW Genesee Street. (WWW) From here, the creek extends south to its source at Roxhill Park, 3.5 miles away.

To the Genesee Stairs (207 steps up): Once you've climbed the stairs up from Longfellow Creek, turn left onto SW Genesee Street and walk east. On the right, just before the stoplight, note Delridge Skatepark, which opened in late 2011. (WWW) Genesee ends here, so take the crosswalk over to the other side of Delridge Way, and head up the Genesee stairs (2).

To your right is a large old brick building, the former Cooper School. It's in the National Register of Historic Places and is a Seattle Landmark. Today, this striking building houses the Youngstown Cultural Arts Center, which hosts youth arts education and has live/work spaces for low-income artists. Like several other Seattle schools designed during World War I, it was built in the

ABOUT LONGFELLOW CREEK

Seattle Parks considers Longfellow Creek to be one of only three major "free-flowing" streams in Seattle—it's exposed to daylight along two-thirds of its length. The creek begins at the newly restored wetlands of Roxhill Park and flows 4 miles north, emptying into the Duwamish River just after passing beneath the Nucor Steel plant near the beginning of this route. Though Longfellow Creek is naturally a year-round stream, its flow can increase dramatically, as it provides stormwater drainage for much of West Seattle.

Like Thornton Creek (see walk 5, "Maple Leaf and Thornton Creek"), the headwaters of Longfellow Creek were originally a wetland and peat bog. Beginning in 2000, volunteers removed old fill and invasive vegetation and planted more than 250,000 native wetland plants in Roxhill Park. This huge citizen effort has increased the water storage capacity at the headwaters, which dampens corrosive high flows during storms. This also improved living conditions for downstream creek-dwellers, such as salmon fry.

In the section you're walking through, huge efforts have been made to plant native vegetation alongside the creek, providing shade and protection from overhead fish predators. Logs have been placed in the streambed to provide additional shelter, slow flows, and help preserve the gravel beds used for fish spawning. These efforts appear to be working: since 1999, volunteers for the King County Salmon Watcher program have monitored Longfellow Creek and have consistently spotted coho and chum salmon, and occasionally chinook salmon and cutthroat trout.

View east from Charlestown stairs

Renaissance Revival style, characterized by a balanced facade with smooth walls, a low-pitched roof, and strong horizontal bands between floors. A severe lack of materials during World War I forced a simplicity that adds bulk and gives this building a large presence in the neighborhood known today as North Delridge (formerly Youngstown).

Continue up the Genesee stairs, with views across the Delridge Valley behind you. **WWW** At the end of the first flight, 23rd Avenue SW comes in from the left. Once past 23rd you start up a much newer second flight, refurbished in the spring of 2011. It ends with another street coming in from your left, 22nd Avenue SW. Just beyond is the third flight of the Genesee stairs, the oldest section of all. At the top, continue up a short street-end to 21st Avenue SW, then turn left.

To the Andover Stairs (72 steps up): As you walk north on 21st through the Pigeon Point neighborhood, you'll be following the top line of the ridge to its northern tip. Between houses you'll catch glimpses of the Downtown skyline, slightly to the right. Continue along 21st until you reach a street sign for Andover on the right. Here, SW Andover is nothing but stairway (3); turn right and take it up, just a couple of houses shy of 20th Avenue SW. Turn left onto 20th and continue walking north until you reach SW Charlestown Street.

Here, you have a choice: take a brief excursion for a potential view from the northern tip of Pigeon Point (depending on the season), or immediately turn right onto Charlestown and head toward your descent down the eastern slope of Pigeon Point.

Pigeon Point Views and Charlestown Stairs (228 steps down): For that brief side excursion, head left from 20th Avenue SW onto Charlestown for a few feet, then take a quick right, back onto 20th Avenue. It dead-ends within just a few houses, and this is where you might be rewarded with great views to the north, depending on the season. Ideally, you'll see the giant orange ship-loading cranes at Terminal 5 and the waters of Elliott Bay, Puget Sound, and the Olympic Mountains beyond. **WWW** Return to SW Charlestown Street and turn left.

Walk east on SW Charlestown just past 19th Avenue SW. Straight ahead is the top of the Charlestown stairs (4), which take a sidelong route down the flank of Pigeon Point. At the first landing you'll see West Marginal Way below, the West Seattle Bridge and the Duwamish River, and possibly the Cascade Mountains in the distance. This is the gritty eastern border of the Pigeon Point neighborhood.

Midway down the Charlestown stairs you may notice bird guano at certain times of year, spotting the stairs and the flanking blackberry bushes. If you look up cautiously (keeping in mind the guano) you might see blue herons roosting high up in the trees.

At the bottom, turn left onto the sidewalk/bikeway. This is a busy bicycle commuter route, so whether alone or in a group, stay together and to the right, always leaving space for bikes coming up fast!

It's a somewhat complicated bicycle/pedestrian interchange here. In general, keep left at all Y intersections, staying on the path that travels highest along the slope. Your goal is to walk beneath the West Seattle Bridge, curving gradually to the left around the northern base of Pigeon Point. To the west, framed by the columns of the West Seattle Bridge, you'll look out on Terminal 5 and the Nucor Steel plant that greets everybody entering and leaving West Seattle. **WWW** A steel mill has operated on this site since the Seattle Steel Company opened in 1905.

Back via Another Set of Charlestown Stairs (46 steps down): Just as your circuit around the base of Pigeon Point is complete, you'll arrive at a final fork in the pedestrian/bicycle path. Again take the left side, heading uphill into the residential area. You'll soon arrive at a charming garden and an obelisk with a message of welcome to Pigeon Point. **WWW**

Once you pass the obelisk, cross over to the right side of the street. About three lots down, look for a path leading directly away from the street into what looks like a vacant lot. This carries to the top of a short set of stairs (5), along the unused right-of-way for SW Charlestown Street. At the bottom, turn left onto the sidewalk that parallels busy Delridge Way.

It gets noisy along this final stretch of the walk, which reflects the status of Delridge Way as a major artery, and the industrial nature of the area. Follow the sidewalk to the next lighted crosswalk, at SW Andover Street. From here you can cross over and check out one of the nearby cafes, or return to your starting place.

20 Mount Baker

A stairway walk in the northern Mount Baker neighborhood leaves lasting impressions. There's gracious old Dose Terrace stairway, with its scroll-like balcony overlooking Lake Washington and Lake Washington Boulevard. Elsewhere on the route, Colman Park's forested path rises up from the lake to meet a classic Olmsted-era tunnel portal, its retro curves accented by thick,

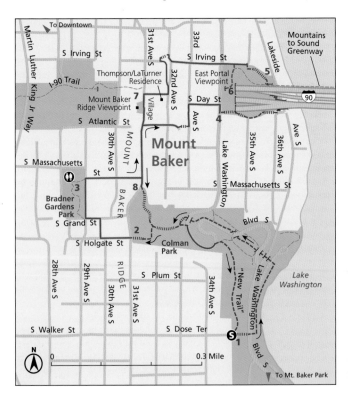

bright-green moss. Up in the neighborhood, Bradner Gardens Park dazzles with a colorful mix of art, P-Patch, and play.

There are vistas you'll see nowhere else. Atop the East Portal Viewpoint over I-90 on Mount Baker Ridge, cars zoom in and out of the tunnel below and onto the floating bridge, with the Cascades and Mount Rainier looming on the horizon. Steps away on the other side of the ridge, there's a perfectly sited new pedestrian viewpoint tucked into the small commercial village. From there the view west is spectacularly framed by the old VA hospital, crowning Beacon Hill, and by Smith Tower, at the southern border of Downtown. You can see all the way out to Puget Sound and the Olympics, through the gap left by the old Dearborn Regrade.

Every stairway walk assumes different aspects throughout the seasons, but this one seems even more affected. In summer there's a sense of mystery and discovery, when thickly shaded woods can suddenly open to reveal a carefully tended P-Patch garden in a quiet ravine. In winter, the bare trees reveal more of the immediate surroundings and even yield tantalizing glimpses beyond, like the blue-gray flashes of Lake Washington you'll see as you contour along the south slope of Colman Park.

In Mount Baker we also found ourselves drawn to the stories of how, a century and more ago, key individuals made local contributions to a city of burgeoning boulevards and parks. In recent years new generations have stepped forward in Mount Baker—not just to preserve and refurbish what has become old, but also to create new and exciting public spaces and works of art.

Length:	**2.4 miles**
Walking Time:	1 hour 30 minutes
Steps Down:	569
Steps Up:	372
Kid-Friendly:	You can adapt this walk for kids by just taking the Dose Terrace stairs down to the beach, where you can wander a bit before heading back up. There are restrooms not too far south of the stairs, halfway up the Mount Baker Park trail. Another kid-friendly variation could start from Bradner Gardens Park, which has parking, a restroom, and lots of whimsical sites to explore (including the restroom!). From there it's just a short walk to 31st Avenue S and its two stairway entrances to Colman Park, at either S Grand Street or S Holgate Street. You can take one of those stairways down to the Colman Park P-Patch and either turn back or meander toward the lake as far as you like. Take the other set of stairs back up to exit, turning this into a very doable, fun "lollipop" loop.

Cafes/Pubs: At Mount Baker Ridge village on 31st, between S Day and S Atlantic streets, Repast Bakery and Cafe is open during daytime hours. Mioposto is a good pizza place south of this route, at 36th Avenue S and S McClellan Street. It's very walkable from the start/end of this route, right near Mount Baker Park. A French and an Italian restaurant are also located in the village, open for dinner only.

Getting There: This walk begins at S Dose Terrace just east of 34th Avenue S. If you're driving, take any of the main Rainier Valley streets south of I-90 (Martin Luther King Jr. Way; 23rd Avenue S; or Rainier Avenue South). Then turn east onto S Walker Street, which becomes S Dose Terrace just past 31st. There's streetside parking near S Dose Terrace and 34th. If you're taking the bus, Metro Transit Route 14 stops near 31st and Dose Terrace and runs between Mount Baker and west Capitol Hill via the International District and Downtown.

Looking back on the stylish Dose Terrace stairs

A DOSE OF MOUNT BAKER HISTORY

Charles P. Dose (pronounced "Doe-see") was one of the real estate developers who created the Mount Baker neighborhood. He owned 40 acres in this area, 10 of them located along the Dose Terrace stairs going all the way up to 31st Avenue S. He platted these as the "Dose Addition" to Seattle. Another company platted a larger, 130-acre sub-division to the south called the "Mount Baker Addition." Both developments were envisioned as an exclusive, parklike residential district for Seattle's professional class. Highly respected planners were recruited for street layout and landscape design, including engineer George Cotterill, who also designed Interlaken Boulevard and other bicycle paths that were incorporated into the Olmsted firm's grand designs (see walk 14, "The Olmsted Vision").

The Mount Baker developments shared Olmsted's "city beautiful" vision, and in 1908 they were added to an updated boulevard plan. Hunter Boulevard, Mount Baker Boulevard, and Mount Baker Park, as well as Colman Park with Lake Washington Boulevard running through it, are all products of the plan. On the side, John C. Olmsted convinced Charles Dose to donate land and build his namesake Dose Terrace steps as a fitting complement to garden-like Lake Washington Boulevard.

The 24 acres of Colman Park are also rife with Olmsted contributions, from its original 1903 concept as part of the boulevard system to the ornamental bridges constructed in 1909 and a comprehensive plan for plantings and paths, completed in 1910. Engineer James M. Colman also played multiple historical roles here and elsewhere (see walk 15, "Downtown"). Most importantly, in 1910 his estate donated a large parcel of property to the park, which was renamed in his honor.

Dose Terrace Stairs (138 steps down): From S Dose Terrace and 34th Avenue S, walk east to the head of the Dose Terrace stairs (1). **WWW** Before heading down, notice the timber steps and path heading onto the hillside to the left; your walk returns via this recently built path, which traverses Colman Park's wooded southern hillside.

Brass letters at the top of the stairs announce "DOSE TERRACE." **WWW** Head down the stairs, which frame great views across Lake Washington. At the bottom, there's a landing from which the stairs split into two curving final flights.

Cross over Lake Washington Boulevard S at the crosswalk for more views over the beach and across the lake. **WWW** It's also a good place to turn back for a view of the dramatic split final flight and scroll-like base of the Dose Terrace stairway. With thick summer foliage, the upper stairs can seem to vanish into

Colman Park: up to the Fourth Tunnel

the slope; in winter the whole impressive length of the stairs stands out. From here you can also see the northern border of Mount Baker Park, just a few yards south. If you have time, it's a fun side excursion.

Through Colman Park via the Holgate Stairs (244 steps up): From the Dose Terrace stairs walk north on the sidewalk, next to the lake. A generous thicket of shrubs and trees soon screens the water from view. This stretch is one of the few places on Lake Washington that still has the kind of well-established shoreline habitat that salmon need for cover and forage. It's common to see waterfowl of various kinds here, as well as turtles and muskrats.

As you walk along the sidewalk, Lake Washington Boulevard angles up the hill a bit. In its place a long driveway appears, running by your side to a parking area ahead.

The thicket to your right soon morphs into an open grassy area, with view benches and a waterside promenade. Keep going a few more steps on the sidewalk. Just before you reach the parking area, look left for a tunnel, then turn up the asphalt path leading to it. You'll pass through this tunnel and another one in quick succession: first under Lakeside Avenue S, then under Lake Washington Boulevard.

After the second tunnel, keep straight on, past an asphalt walkway on the left and some timber steps heading up to the right. The walkway narrows and changes to gravel. From here you'll encounter many widely placed timber steps as you climb to the top of Colman Park.

The path takes you under a third tunnel, then briefly follows alongside meandering Lake Washington Boulevard before breaking away to the fourth and final tunnel. Just before that tunnel, take one of two short flights of stairs on either side. There are low-lying benches set into either side of the tunnel entrance; a deep layer of soft moss covers their sitting surfaces, giving this Olmsted-era antique a look of debauched elegance. `WWW`

Coming out on the other side, a gentle slope leads up to a low curving wall, which makes stepping out of the tunnel feel a little like stepping onto an amphitheater stage. `WWW` The path itself turns sharply left, pointing up at the "frog pond" tucked into the base of the hillside. Two surface channels carry water down to this little artificial pond. To manage chronic flooding, the pond was dug and the area around it was graded. Both the pond and channels were planted with native vegetation. This is meant to slow storm runoff surges and entice native species, including frogs and other amphibians, to live here.

Continue up the trail and numerous timber pathway steps. You'll pass the Colman Park P-Patch community garden, which used to be a parks nursery. This is a glorious early-morning-sun kind of place, especially during growing season. Just above the P-Patch, a bench marks a fork in the trail. Turn onto the left fork (after a few more adventures outside Colman Park you'll return down the other fork). After 61 more timber pathway steps you reach the concrete Holgate stairs (2), whose striking angular lines announce that you're about to enter a different world. `WWW`

Once you've climbed the 56 steps of the Holgate stairs to exit Colman Park, you'll find yourself standing on the sidewalk next to 31st Avenue S. Take the crosswalk straight ahead onto S Holgate Street and into the next, residential phase of your exploration.

To Bradner Gardens Park: Walk west on Holgate for one block, then turn right onto 30th Avenue S. The second home on the east side of 30th features a "stairway to heaven," a very colorful tile installation at the bottom of a set of

A GARDEN OF EARTHLY DELIGHTS

Bradner Gardens Park is an important focal point for residents of the north Mount Baker neighborhood and a must-see for curious urban explorers. A stroll here gets you nice views of the city skyline and many other visual delights and surprises. An ornamental garden runs along part of the perimeter path, offering a variety of themed plots, like "Winter Interest" or "Butterfly-Hummingbird," and a couple of seating areas to relax and enjoy those butterflies. There are P-Patch gardens and a beekeeping area too, and all of it is pesticide-free. There's a small basketball court, a picnic shelter (WWW), and a whimsical play tractor. A modernist structure at the north end houses a restroom and conference room. There's cool art everywhere.

The restroom is an attraction in itself. The walls are covered with shiny tiles and crockery shards in a colorful, lyrical rendition of the insects and plants that make these gardens their home. (WWW) Joyce Moty, one of the mosaic's three creators (WWW), says their intent was to make an attractive public facility that says "everybody deserves a quality experience." It's been open 24/7 since 2003—and, with one minor exception, vandalism-free. Before the park was built, the City almost divested this 1.6-acre property. Without the help of neighborhood visionaries and volunteers it would have become a high-end residential development. You can learn about the unique story of this park at www.bradnergardenspark.org.

private steps. (WWW) We recognize the Virgin of Guadalupe and Lord Ganesha; hopefully, readers can tell us about the other religious figures embedded there.

After walking one block on 30th, turn left onto S Grand Street. At the northwest corner of the next block you'll see the sign for Bradner Gardens Park (3).

To the Atlantic and Day Street Stairs (229 steps down): After your exploration of Bradner Gardens Park (see "A Garden of Earthly Delights"), exit from the eastern entry arbor. It's one of three arbors that, like the "Stairs to Nowhere" (see walk 7, "University of Washington"), were designed, fabricated, and installed by UW architecture students. The school regularly undertakes such projects for nonprofits around town to give students hands-on experience while adding to the community.

Turn left at Bradner Gardens Park's exit and walk slightly downhill along 29th Avenue S. Turn right at the next street, S Massachusetts Street, and walk two blocks to 31st Avenue S. Cross 31st at the crosswalk, carefully; the visibility along this arterial is limited to the right, where 31st curves. The northern stairway (8) down into Colman Park is a few steps south. Later you'll return to those steps. For now, turn left onto the sidewalk and follow it north to the next block, S Atlantic Street. Walk east on Atlantic for a block until it ends at a "DEAD END" sign. This is your cue for adventure!

Keep walking down what looks like a long driveway, and soon you'll notice the top of a handrail peeking up on the left, guiding you down a short flight of stairs followed by a narrow walkway. Tread carefully here, as the asphalt can be covered with damp leaves or moss, and it's steep. You'll reach a final set of stairs on this passage that puts you down on 33rd Avenue S, though there's no street sign.

Turn left onto 33rd and then right in one block, onto S Day Street. At the intersection there are very nice views of the lake, Bellevue, and the Cascades; the views expand to the north as you continue down Day Street.

At the bottom, Day Street ends at Lake Washington Boulevard. Look across the boulevard, a few feet to the left. Here you'll see dual plaques commemorating Lacey V. Murrow, elder brother of newsman Edward R. Murrow. The elder Murrow was state director of highways when the I-90 floating bridge was built; the plaques overlook the bridge.

From Day Street, cross over Lake Washington Boulevard, which is fairly quiet on this stretch. For added safety, we recommend you take the crosswalk from the north side of Day. Once across, turn right and head south along the sidewalk. The sidewalk bends as the street briefly widens to accommodate a parking lane. Where the street narrows again, find the short stretch of sidewalk on the left. It leads directly to your next, long stretch of stairs.

There are three sections of Day Street stairs (4): the upper section, which is behind you and not on this route; the middle section, which you're about to head down; and a lower section, which picks up after the middle section bottoms out.

The middle Day stairs emerge onto 35th Avenue S. Straight ahead is a curving walkway, which you'll follow to the lower Day stairs. Directly to your left, the street ends in a cul-de-sac, right beside I-90. The cars rush eastbound out of the tunnel here, and the noise level is high.

Ahead of you is a curving walkway and plaza, with the kind of Machine Age architecture perfectly in tune with the look of the tunnel entrance. Even the light standards have a distinctive Marvin the Martian look! **WWW** Cross the street and walk around the plaza, which curves close to I-90 just before reaching the top of the lower Day stairs.

After 94 steps down, the stairway leaves you just below the level of I-90. There's a somewhat complicated mix of roads and paths here; just turn left onto a broad asphalt lane planted with wooden bollards, and start walking under I-90.

(Although not a part of the main route, from this point it's possible to diverge a bit and cross busy Lakeside Avenue. From there you can explore South Day Street Park, a boat put-in spot and pocket park. It provides a unique shoreline perspective, right under the bridge.)

Mount Baker Viewpoint Park

To the Lower Irving Stairs (77 steps up): After you walk beneath the eastbound lanes of I-90, continue past the emergency access road heading up to the left, usually blocked by a chainlink gate. As you continue under the westbound lanes, you'll see the lower Irving stairs ahead (5).

The stairs are one route up to the I-90 bike path which is part of the Mountains to Sound Greenway (it accommodates pedestrians too). Between the top of these steps and the East Portal Viewpoint ahead, be extra-vigilant for speeding bicycles! The stairs have runnels that bicyclists use to wheel their mounts up and down. **WWW** Heading west, the bike path ducks under the I-90 Lid before popping out on the far side of Mount Baker Ridge. Going east, it crosses the lake to Mercer Island, right next to the westbound lanes.

At the top of the lower Irving stairs, angle a few steps to your right, where S Irving Street and 35th Avenue S meet. From there, follow the sidewalk to the left, up Irving and away from 35th.

East Portal Viewpoint and the Upper Irving Stairs (39 steps up): Once on S Irving Street, you'll quickly pull even with a bicycle driveway on the left marked by a bollard standing upright in the middle. This is another entrance to the I-90 bike path, so beware of speeding bikes as you turn up this little lane to the East Portal Viewpoint (6), just ahead. From there you'll get stellar views across the lake and south toward Mount Rainier, with traffic whizzing in and out of the tunnels beneath your feet.

Returning to Irving Street, continue up the steep hill past Lake Washington Boulevard, and then past 33rd Avenue S. You'll notice that 32nd Avenue ahead seems blocked by a concrete wall; this marks the site of the upper Irving stairs.

As you get closer to the wall, you'll see the base of the upper Irving stairs to the right. They make a quick zigzag, ending up parallel to Irving at the top. Here, cross Irving and take the curve around to the uphill lane of 32nd Avenue, walking south.

Mount Baker Ridge Vistas: After a few steps, the uphill and downhill lanes of 32nd Avenue come back together. There are fantastic views across a vacant lot, over the I-90 floating bridge and beyond. Birds of prey, like the peregrine falcon we've seen perched on a bordering tree, also seem to like the open views.

At this point you're standing atop Mount Baker Ridge, which is narrow enough to provide exceptional east and west vistas just steps apart from each other.

At the next junction where 32nd meets S Day Street, look to the house on the southwest corner. It's the restored 1894 Victorian Queen Anne structure known as the Thompson LaTurner Residence, a Seattle Landmark that's also listed on the National Register of Historic Places. The three-story octagonal turret and the wraparound veranda are the most prominent physical features. The original

A SINGULAR VIEW FROM MOUNT BAKER RIDGE

Mount Baker Ridge Viewpoint is a broad viewing deck that juts out over a steep slope, providing a brilliant view to the west. Two prominent landmarks to be seen are the VA building at the north end of Beacon Hill, and Smith Tower at the south end of Downtown. Between them is a large gap, through which you can view Puget Sound and the Olympics. That gap is the result of the Dearborn Regrade, which between 1907 and 1912 removed more than 100 feet of Beacon Hill soil and used it as landfill to create Harbor Island. Today, Jose Rizal Bridge crosses the gap from the north end of Beacon Hill to the International District. Importantly, the regrade also connected Downtown to the Rainier Valley. This opened up a previously hemmed-in Seattle and transformed the town into a viable metropolis.

Another notable feature of the viewpoint is its "contemporary Stonehenge" function (see walk 17, "Solstice Park," for a different version). Look for seven pairs of upright polished basalt stones scattered around the deck. Each pair has a small gap or slot in the middle; line them up with a corresponding slot in the deck railing beyond, and you'll see where the sun will set at a given solstice or equinox. The park opened on March 20, 2009: spring equinox.

owner, William Thompson, grew up in Georgia, fought for the Confederate army as a youth, and went on to become general counsel for the Great Northern Railway. After he died, this house was used variously as a sanitarium and rooming house.

From 32nd turn right onto S Day. At the next block, cross 31st Avenue S. Turn left onto the sidewalk and then, past the first building and just off the street to your right, you'll find magnificent Mount Baker Ridge Viewpoint Park (7; see "A Singular View from Mount Baker Ridge").

Continue south past the viewpoint and the commercial village, passing restaurants and a bakery on the way. Cross 31st at the crosswalk at S Massachusetts Street, then turn right to continue along the east side of 31st. Just as the street curves, you'll find the signed top of a stairway (8) leading back down to the Colman Park P-Patch.

Return via Colman Park Hillside (202 steps down, 12 steps up): Head down 70 concrete stairs into Colman Park. When streetcar tracks were removed all over the city, the old rail materials were recycled. These stair-treads are made from the concrete slabs that used to lie between streetcar rails—two stacked slabs per tread. Perhaps these stair trails come from the old streetcar line that used to serve the commercial village you just passed through.

The concrete stairs turn to timber pathway steps as they skirt a wooden fence and descend around a curve. At the familiar junction marked by a bench just

OLD TRAIL, NEW TRAIL

In 2002 a city worker discovered 120 trees freshly cut down in an isolated area of Colman Park. It turned out to be the work of a crew under the command of retired federal judge Jerome Farris, carried out on park property just beyond his fence. The judge claimed miscommunication with his workers and ultimately settled with the city for $618,000.

Neighborhood activists, led by members of the Mount Baker Community Club, fought to make sure the payment went to restoring the park. As replanting and restoration work began, an old Olmsted-designed trail was rediscovered and cleared. It led into the forested south hillside of the park before turning back to the north end, some 650 feet short of the Dose Terrace stairs at the southern border.

The rediscovered and rebuilt trail made a significant section of the park newly accessible to the public, but it also spurred another dream: to build a spur all the way to the Dose Terrace stairs. This would open up the whole park to walkers, and provide a trail link with Mount Baker Park to the south. You traverse this new trail on the final leg of your walk.

above the P-Patch, step back onto the same trail you came up—but this time heading downhill.

As you approach the tunnel and the road, bear right on the trail, away from the tunnel and toward Lake Washington Boulevard. Walk carefully along the curving pavement for less than 200 paces, where you'll encounter a sharp hairpin to the left marked by a steel guardrail. Turn off the road just before the guardrail, onto a trail that carries you into the forested hillside.

The initial part of this trail is a restored section of one of the original Olmsted-planned trails that until recently was lost and overgrown. About halfway to the Dose Terrace stairs, that path turns downhill toward the lake, while you go straight ahead on a new trail (see "Old Trail, New Trail"). The new trail follows the contour of the hillside. It eventually works its way to a final few timber steps that join the top of the Dose Terrace stairs (1).

21 Deadhorse Canyon and Rainier Beach

The name "Deadhorse Canyon" brings up visions of squinty-eyed desperados and desert hideouts—unusual images for a Pacific Northwest location. One theory is that during logging days, felled trees sometimes landed too awkwardly on the canyon slope to be easily grappled to the mill below. These trees were simply left behind as "dead horses." Another theory is that someone's horse actually did wander off and die around here.

Whatever the real story, we do know this canyon on the south end of Lake Washington was thoroughly logged, like almost everywhere else around the Sound. Taylor Sawmill operated at its mouth until the early 1900s, processing logs from Deadhorse Canyon and other sources around the lake. When the logging petered out, the tract around Taylor Creek was sold for a residential development to be called Lakeridge. The canyon itself wasn't suitable for building homes, so in 1947 it was deeded over to Seattle Parks.

Today, 35-acre Lakeridge Park encompasses most of the canyon, and the City and the Friends of Deadhorse Canyon have worked to restore native plants and trees. It's now a second-growth wonderland, shady-green and accessible, a repository of native flora and fauna. A pair of bald eagles are said to nest here, and pileated woodpeckers and ospreys are frequently seen.

Taylor Creek runs the length of Deadhorse Canyon, emptying into Lake Washington. In late winter when sight lines are clear, the strong-running stream looks impressive from the bridge above. You might not recognize it as the same creek at the height of the dry summer season when it runs much more quietly,

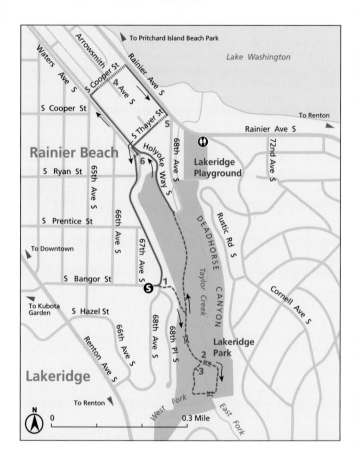

leafy undergrowth screening it from view. Taylor Creek once hosted a salmon run, and culverts in the higher reaches of the canyon have been modified to encourage salmon migration; it's hoped that when the final barrier is removed from the creek's mouth, salmon will return.

The walk through Deadhorse Canyon covers 127 scattered timber pathway steps. The route turns up and then down the canyon, within the precincts of Lakeridge Park. You'll eventually exit the canyon to walk through the Rainier Beach neighborhood, following residential streets and stairways that provide marvelous south Lake Washington views. The highlight of this part of the walk is the Cooper stairs, a major Seattle stairway, with 218 alluring steps.

The walk itself is short—around an hour—so you may have time to visit other Rainier Beach destinations. A premier attraction is 20-acre Kubota Garden, a labor of decades on the part of the Kubota family. You can spend hours strolling through the intricate landscaping, exotic plantings, and subtle water features, and even enjoy a picnic on the expansive lawn. Another neighborhood destination is historic Pritchard Island Beach, where you can explore paths through 4 acres of restored wetland, enjoy the beach and bathhouse, and avail yourself of ADA-compliant restrooms.

Length:	**1.8 miles**
Walking Time:	About 1 hour
Steps Down:	307
Steps Up:	120
Kid-Friendly:	Kids who can handle the initial steep, but maintained, gravel trail down into Lakeridge Park will love the canyon, which can be explored as an easy in-and-out walk. Kubota Garden makes a wonderful walk-around and picnic spot.
Cafes/Pubs:	There's a shopping center on Rainier Avenue northwest of the walk. Pizzeria Pulcinella, on Rainier Avenue at the mouth of Deadhorse Canyon, offers exceptional authentic Neapolitan-style pies (call for hours). Kubota Garden is a perfect picnic setting, as is Pritchard Island Beach.

Getting There: If driving, park on S Bangor Street, east of 67th Avenue S. Metro Transit Route 106 runs from Downtown, with a stop on Bangor at Renton Avenue S, within 0.2 mile of the walk's start/end.

The first part of this route involves walking down a rather steep gravel pathway; wear walking or hiking shoes with good traction.

A Hidden Lakeridge Park Entrance: From S Bangor Street, head east until it ends at a complicated four-way intersection. Waters Avenue S comes in on your left; 68th Avenue S intersects from the right, and 68th Place S runs up ahead of you before curving sharply right. Continue straight ahead and over the near curb, just left of a couple of green electrical boxes, into what at first looks like somebody's side yard. Just after you pass to the left of the "LAKERIDGE PARK ESTATES" sign, you'll be on a gravel path (1) that leads around a house, into the park, and down into the canyon. This path is a recent project of the Friends of Deadhorse Canyon.

After an initial steep descent, you'll come to a junction with the main path leading up and down the canyon, on the west side of Taylor Creek. Turn right, up canyon, and soon after that you'll cross a fairly long wooden bridge across the junction of two small side ravines. At this point you're fully immersed in a green garden of cedar, hemlock, Indian plum, and countless other native plants. **WWW**

Looking back up the Cooper stairs

Inside Deadhorse Canyon (38 steps up, 89 steps down): After crossing the first bridge, continue along the west slope. Watch for another path off to the right; you'll be returning that way after making a loop at the head of the canyon. The path makes a sharp jog around a tree just before reaching a second bridge (2), this one across Taylor Creek and over to the east side of the canyon. **WWW** A few steps beyond the bridge, the trail takes you up a few more timber stairs, around a corner and on up the canyon.

The trail runs only briefly along the east side of the canyon before turning right and toward a bridge back across Taylor Creek. Before you reach the bridge, you'll pass a small side trail to the left; it meanders briefly up the southeast arm of the head of the canyon before petering out.

Taylor Creek's two upstream tributaries come together just off the left side of the bridge. The tributary coming from the southwest arm of the canyon is fed by a spring farther up the wooded slopes of the park, more or less ahead of you. The other tributary originates in Skyway Park, to the south.

Once you're across the bridge and back on the west side of the canyon, the route turns north, heading down toward the canyon mouth.

Susanna Stodden Memorial and Canyon Exit: Here the path clambers up and down a bit until you encounter a series of steps, mostly heading downhill. Your initial bridge comes back into view, this time from the opposite side. You'll soon reach a junction and start back down the trail the way you came. Before you get there, you'll see a rest stop just off the trail to the right (3). It has a comfortable viewing bench and a memorial plaque dedicated to Susanna Stodden, a volunteer and advocate for Deadhorse Canyon. **WWW**

From this quiet spot, continue down the trail toward the park exit. There are a few more pathway timber steps on the way, but the main stairway event on this walk is still ahead, outside the park. As you walk, watch for a "mysterious," moss-covered monolith on the left of the trail. **WWW** The park trail ends with a street—right at a hairpin turn where 68th Avenue S on the right turns into Holyoke Way S, on the left. Turn left to walk up and out of the canyon.

After you climb out of the canyon, continue along in the same general direction, as Waters Avenue S joins in from behind you on the left (on your return leg, you'll be taking Waters in that direction). After merging with Waters, continue your generally northwest course, past S Thayer Street on your right, to S Cooper Street.

The Cooper Stairs (218 steps down): Turn right and walk a short distance on Cooper. The street ends in a beautiful set of stairs (4). They extend down to Rainier Avenue S, with fantastic views of Lake Washington and Mercer Island. **WWW**

When you finally arrive at the bottom of the Cooper stairs, turn right onto the sidewalk next to Rainier Avenue S. The street is busy and noisy, but you'll only be on it for a couple of hundred yards. The sidewalk is generally good, although just before it meets S Thayer, you may have to bat away a few blackberry vines.

Thayer Stairs (53 steps up): Turn right onto S Thayer Street, which immediately carries you up a set of 53 stairs (5). The stairs end in a concrete pathway, which in turn becomes a full-blown street. Continue ahead for a block and a half, until Thayer runs into Waters Avenue S.

Holyoke Stairs (29 steps up): At this point Waters Avenue is a divided road. The lane directly in front of you carries traffic north and to your right, as marked by the "ONE WAY" sign. Turn left here up the sidewalk, walking briefly against the flow of traffic.

As you walk southeast along Waters, you'll approach a Y junction where Waters turns up to the right and Holyoke runs down to the left, where you came up from Lakeridge Park. Here you can see the Holyoke stairs ahead to the right (6). It's the shortest concrete stairway of your walk, and the last. **WWW** At the top of Holyoke stairs, turn left, onto the upper section of Waters Avenue S.

After a half block, the separate lanes of Waters merge into a single right-of-way, just past S Ryan Street. Continue ahead on Waters for two blocks until you reach the junction with S Bangor Street, where you originally entered Deadhorse Canyon. This ends the route, but there are other nearby neighborhood destinations you may want to visit while you're here (see "Option: Side Trip to Kubota Garden" and "Option: Side Trip to Pritchard Island Beach Park"). Either of them makes a nice picnic spot.

In addition, check out the book website for pictures and descriptions of the Rainier Beach neighborhood's "neglected stairs." Unfortunately, there are several potentially wonderful stairways and paths here that have fallen into disuse and disrepair. **WWW**

Option: Side Trip to Kubota Garden

Twenty-acre Kubota Garden is a Seattle Landmark and a wonderful place to visit any time of year. **WWW** It's filled with an immense range of artfully placed exotic trees and shrubs, and its appearance changes constantly with the seasons. A waterfall tumbles over a rock garden at the western edge to feed several streams and ponds, some of them crossed by paths of huge flat rocks, others spanned by arching bridges. Paths weave through the garden, giving visitors access to multiple angles and hidden nooks.

Kubota Garden is owned and maintained by Seattle Parks, but prior to 1987 it was owned by the Japanese-American Kubota family. The garden started as a 5-acre property purchased in 1927 by the immigrant family patriarch, Fujitaro Kubota. He established his landscape design reputation through projects like Bloedel Reserve on Bainbridge Island and the gardens at Seattle Pacific University. Kubota built his business offices, display center, and home on this land. With subsequent purchases it also slowly grew into the elder Kubota's personal monument to Japanese-inspired garden design.

The garden is close to the start/finish of this stairway walk. To drive there, head west on S Bangor Street. After five or six blocks, turn right at the light onto Renton Avenue S. The garden entrance is less than a mile down Renton on the left, at the junction with 55th Avenue S. ◆

Option: Side Trip to Pritchard Island Beach Park

This is a community center for wetlands environmental education, a wildlife refuge, and a place where Seattleites can enjoy nature close to home. Before settlement by white people, the former island here, near the south Lake Washington shore, was home to a group of Puget-Salish people. They called it *tleelh-chus* or "Little Island." In 1855 these first people were removed to reservations, and the island came into the possession of A. B. Young, to be called Young's Island until it took on the name of its next owner, Alfred Pritchard. Pritchard platted a street (today's Island Drive S) and started its residential development.

When the lake's surface level fell with the opening of the Ship Canal, the slough between the island and shore was transformed into a muddy bottomland, and the island disappeared. The area was drained, and the City eventually acquired it by condemnation in 1934. Seattle City Light began using the land as a nursery before finally handing it over to Seattle Parks. In 1996 the parks department began working with the newly formed Friends of Pritchard Beach Park to restore the wetlands and build an urban nature education center. With paths through 4 acres of restored wetland, Pritchard Island Beach lets us glimpse how our local lakeside habitats might have looked before logging and development. **WWW** The park is located in Rainier Beach, about 2 miles north of this walk's starting place, at S Grattan Street and 55th Avenue S. Beach, bathhouse, and restrooms are available. ♦

22 Lakewood–Seward Park

We still remember the excitement of discovering the leafy, secretive stairs hidden at the Ferdinand street-end, and the magical feeling of being immersed in the heart of this beautiful lakeside neighborhood, plunging along obscure back pathways and slopes.

As with the Laurelhurst and Madrona walks, Lake Washington is also a big presence, visually and historically. The development of both the Lakewood and Seward Park neighborhoods (typically lumped together as "Lakewood-Seward Park") is closely tied to the level of the lake, which fell drastically in 1916. That's covered in more detail in the sidebar "Before Genesee Park".

The main route can be reconfigured in various ways. A more robust version includes the Genesee Park side trip, which adds interesting historical places and details, along with 1.5 miles.

Length:	**1.8 miles (add 1.5 miles with Genesee Park side trip)**
Walking Time:	1 hour (add 45 minutes with Genesee Park side trip)
Steps Down:	174
Steps Up:	207
Kid-Friendly:	Kids might enjoy a shorter version of the main walk, centered around the very cool Ferdinand Street and Angeline Street stairways and the Lake Washington shoreline. Near the start of the main route, from the northeast corner of Lakewood Park, head east on S Angeline Street. Then follow the directions from "To the Angeline Walkway and Stairs," starting with the last paragraph of that section.
Cafes/Pubs:	There's a PCC market and a Caffé Vita at the southwest edge of this route, near where 50th Avenue S turns into Wilson Avenue S going south. For a cozy neighborhood coffee or bite to eat halfway through your walk, try Both Ways Cafe near the bottom of the 48th Avenue stairs on S Genesee Street. Flying Squirrel Pizza is next door, though they're only open after 5 PM.

Getting There: The walk starts at the northwest corner of Lakewood Park, at 50th Avenue S and S Angeline Street. You can park anywhere on the nearby residential streets. By bus, King County Metro Route 50 runs between Alki, Beacon Hill, and Rainier Valley, and stops near the northwest corner of Lakewood Park, at 50th Avenue S and S Angeline Street.

A First Glimpse of the Angeline Stairs (24 steps up): On a sunny day, you'll probably see lots of parents and kids cavorting at Lakewood Playground. From the park's northwest corner, carefully cross 50th Avenue S, a busy arterial, and continue walking west on S Angeline Street.

On the far side of 50th, you'll see the Lakewood Seward Park Community Club, founded in 1910. One block ahead you can see the first set of Angeline stairs (1), which climb a short slope just after you cross 49th. **WWW**

After just 24 steps up, you'll be back on Angeline Street. Continue on Angeline one and a half blocks, turning right onto 47th Avenue S.

To the 47th Avenue Stairs (50 steps up): Walk north two blocks to S Snoqualmie Street. Here, 47th Avenue ends in a stairway at the base of a steep slope (2). **WWW** Head up the stairway and after 50 steps, you'll find yourself on a concrete walkway almost as steep as the steps.

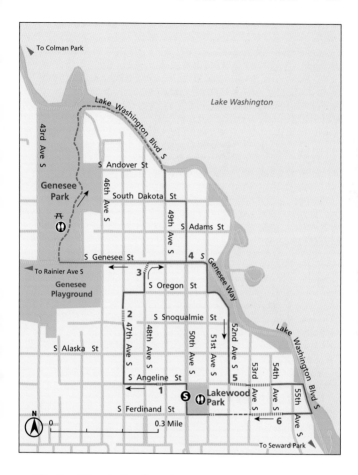

After about 25 yards of walkway, the street starts up again. Continue a half-block farther on 47th Avenue, turning right onto S Oregon Street. After one block, turn left onto 48th Avenue S, heading north.

48th Avenue Stairs to Genesee (43 steps down): As you walk north on 48th Avenue, you'll reach a stairway curving gracefully down to S Genesee Street (3). At the bottom, continue east on the sidewalk toward the next major junction, Genesee and 50th Avenue S (4). At this point, you can take a side trip to Genesee Park (see "Option: Side Trip to Genesee Park").

Option: Side Trip to Genesee Park

From S Genesee Street, it's an easy side trek to Genesee Park and old Wetmore Slough, adding about 45 minutes to your walk.

You can cross S Genesee Street from the base of the 48th Avenue stairs (3), but for safety's sake we strongly recommend that you first head east on Genesee to 50th Avenue S, where you can use the crosswalk (4). Then double back, walking west along the north side of Genesee for five blocks.

You'll see a soccer field on the south side of S Genesee, and then a crosswalk coming across the street to intersect your path from the left. At this point, turn right off the sidewalk, following a park sign and a walkway into Genesee Park. There will be some park outbuildings on your right.

Just past the outbuildings, the walkway curves between seasonally open restrooms and a play structure, and the park itself becomes visible. As you walk through what was a former slough (see "Before Genesee Park" for a history of the park), you'll see a covered picnic structure on the left and beyond that, a perennial garden. You can explore the garden along small side paths, or just skirt it on the right, continuing on the main path.

Keep to the main path until you arrive at the park exit, at Lake Washington Boulevard S. Carefully cross here, then take the walkway curving down toward the water. This scenic walkway continues right alongside the lake.

In less than a quarter mile, cross back over the boulevard to 49th Avenue S (it's safer here than at 50th), walking south for one block. Turn left on S Dakota Street and then right at the next block, onto 50th Avenue S.

After walking two blocks south on 50th Avenue S, you'll be back at the junction with S Genesee (4). Turn left to pick up the route of the main walk at "To the Angeline Walkway and Stairs." ◆

To the Angeline Walkway and Stairs (63 steps down): From the four-way stop at S Genesee Street and 50th Avenue S, walk east one block on Genesee, then turn right onto 51st Ave S as Genesee angles away down the slope toward the lake. After one block on 51st, turn left onto S Oregon Street, which curves toward the lake, then straightens as it joins 52nd Avenue S. From here, the street heads sharply uphill all the way to the Angeline stairs.

At the S Alaska Street junction, look for the retaining wall on your right, which sometimes features neighborhood art "installations." WWW Continue uphill on 52nd. The Angeline walkway and stairs (5) begin on your left, just opposite of where S Angeline Street comes in from the right. Start down a short section of walkway to the head of the first flight of stairs. You'll discover that

Stepping down the 48th Avenue stairs to Genesee

most of the Angeline "stairway" is actually a lovely concrete walkway, tucked between laurel hedges and trees as it runs two blocks down toward the lake.

After traversing the walkway/stairs down to 54th Avenue S, continue on S Angeline Street for a block and a half, until it ends at Lake Washington Boulevard. **WWW** There are crosswalks flanking both sides of Angeline here. After crossing, turn up the sidewalk to the right, following it alongside the lakeshore for about a block. When the sidewalk starts veering toward the lake, look for S Ferdinand Street dropping down the hill from the right and angle to it, across the grass.

BEFORE GENESEE PARK: WETMORE SLOUGH

Before 1916, the surface of Lake Washington was 9 feet higher than it is today. The Ship Canal was opened that year, which lowered the lake and caused profound impacts all around the shore, including here at Genesee Park.

When the lake was higher, today's parkland was well underwater. Wetmore Slough, named after an early landowner, extended south from Lake Washington all the way to where Genesee Street is located today, and west almost all the way to Rainier Avenue in Columbia City. This left a bit of isolated land to the east of the slough, a peninsula jutting north into the lake.

In 1895 ambitious developers planned to dredge the slough and dig a canal through Beacon Hill, connecting Lake Washington, via locks, with the southern part of Elliott Bay. The idea was to transform the slough into a freshwater port for seagoing ships coming in to Seattle. This was attractive to shipowners, partly because fresh water gets rid of organisms that foul a seagoing ship's hull. The canal project was abandoned, though, after various financial, political, and geological setbacks. Soil from the initial excavations was used to help build Harbor Island and fill in the mudflats south of Pioneer Square.

In 1916 when the lake dropped, Wetmore Slough was reduced to a mucky wallow. Between 1945 and 1965, the City of Seattle used the area as landfill, which drew overwhelming populations of rats and gulls. The neighbors were ecstatic when, in 1968, construction started on a park that would eventually cover the landfill, transforming the old slough into a lively bird habitat and a lovely, walkable park. Nowadays, Seattle Audubon Society does monthly bird counts in this park.

The Ferdinand Stairs (133 steps up, 68 steps down): Take the crosswalk to Ferdinand and up to the base of the Ferdinand stairs (6). This next part of the route covers three and a half blocks of tree-lined stairs and walkway. The first section of 90 stairs vaults up the shoulder of the hillside ahead, up to 54th Avenue S.

As you step onto 54th, take a moment to look left (being careful about approaching cars). Someone installed dazzling vintage car bumpers as a sort of railing between their driveway and the street! **WWW**

Above 54th, you'll quickly traverse two flights totaling 43 steps. **WWW** After that your route levels and turns into paved pathway. You'll soon notice a stairway intersecting your own route at right angles, dropping off to your right.

Heading back: up Ferdinand stairs to Lakewood Park

This stairway marks the 53rd Avenue S right-of-way. If you peek down through the trees, you'll see 53rd Avenue below, and Seattle Parks' Lakewood Moorage 0.3 mile away on the shore.

At 52nd Avenue S, the Ferdinand right-of-way switches from pathway to street for just a half block, after which you begin your brief and only downhill section of the Ferdinand stairs, 68 steps in all. At the bottom, Ferdinand becomes a street for good, arriving at Lakewood Park and your starting place.

Option: Side Trip to Seward Park

As the Olmsted firm's 1903 parks plan had it, the Bailey Peninsula would be the southern anchor of a system of parks and boulevards running all the way from Lake Washington to Puget Sound, north of Ballard. In 1911 the City bought the peninsula from the Bailey family, and the firm went to work on plans for a park.

Today, Seward Park has miles of trails throughout the peninsula. It has a swimming beach and picnic and play areas, as well as a wonderful National Audubon Society center that introduces visitors of all ages to local habitat and animal life through multiple events and classes (sewardpark.audubon.org).

The park occupies all 300 acres of the peninsula. The interior is heavily wooded, with about 120 acres at the north end considered to be old-growth forest. Old-growth is defined as forest containing trees that are over 250 years old, with standing snags (i.e., dead trees), large downed logs, and a multilayer canopy. These features make for an incredibly rich biological environment.

To get there from your starting place at Lakewood Park, drive south on 50th Avenue S, which turns into Wilson Avenue S after a block. A half mile from Lakewood Park, turn left onto S Orcas Street. Orcas merges to the right with Lake Washington Boulevard, shortly before the boulevard enters the park (and ends). ◆

23 Burien: Eagle Landing Stairs

This is the shortest route—only 0.4 mile long with just one major set of stairs—but it's one of our favorites. The stairway goes through the middle of a sensitive geological and ecological zone, so it was built with unusual construction methods and has a striking pier-and-girder design. As the stairs angle back and forth down a precipitous slope, they seem to hover above the hillside, protective of the fragile environment below. WWW

Depending on how you count these things, the main Eagle Landing stairway is the fourth longest in the region, at 289 steps. It's a visually stunning concrete-and-steel structure, set down incongruously in a thickly wooded setting. The landscape architect for the park, Ed McLeod, says that while the structure is light on the land, it doesn't try to cover up its essential intrusiveness. We think this complementary mix of straightforwardness and sensitivity makes the stairs an unusually charming vehicle through a beautiful landscape. They also provide

Heading back up the Eagle Landing stairs

valued community access to a pristine beach while minimizing impacts. We're partial to the way the stairs end at the very bottom, as a collapsed semi-wreck that shows what high-tide storms can accomplish by tossing a few battering-ram logs around. Hardier walkers should easily make it down to the beach at low tide, though conditions down there can always change.

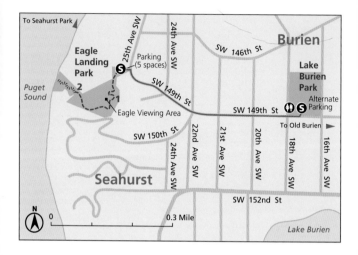

As for the park itself, Eagle Landing Park covers 6 acres of heavily forested ravines and slopes, squeezed between houses north and south, and 2 acres of ecologically valuable tidelands. Yet the park feels like a secluded, almost sacred space. The area was logged in the 1890s, but today Eagle Landing is a wonderful second-growth environment, and volunteers continue to restore native understory vegetation. There are many large trees here, including some 100-year-old Douglas firs. One of them has hosted a bald eagle pair since 1991, lending the park its name. **WWW** There are also western red cedars and big-leaf maples, and the higher and drier slopes support a population of large and healthy madrona trees.

Otters, sea lions, bats, coyotes, and flying squirrels have all been spotted here. Large birds like barred owls, ospreys, great horned owls, and pileated woodpeckers have been tallied, as have many songbirds—up to seventy species in all. Excellent interpretive signs discuss the eagle's life cycle, explain the slide geology underfoot and its effect on habitat, and illustrate how the ecosystems change rapidly from trailhead to water. Eagle Landing Park is a space very much devoted to experiencing and learning about urban nature.

There are just five parking spaces at the park entrance, so keep Lake Burien School Memorial Park in mind as an optional start. It's just east of the route, a 0.5-mile walk through pleasant neighborhoods to the trailhead (see directions under "Getting There").

While you're here, check out pedestrian-friendly Old Burien, a charmingly renewed commercial area that runs east–west along SW 152nd Street, on either side of Ambaum Boulevard. There's a new city hall, library, and town square, plus bookstores, cafes, and other places to browse or snack.

Length:	**0.4 mile (add 0.5 mile each way if parking at Lake Burien Park)**
Walking Time:	30 minutes (add 30 minutes if parking at Lake Burien Park)
Steps Down:	289 (not counting 24 additional timber steps on trail)
Steps Up:	289
Kid-Friendly:	Eagle Landing Park has no place to play or go to the bathroom. But the route is very short, and the stairs have plenty of landings for rest stops. There are good play and restroom facilities at nearby Lake Burien Park.
Cafes/Pubs:	Old Burien has many restaurant, bakery, and cafe opportunities. Two kid-friendly pubs are the Elliott Bay Brewhouse and Mick Kelly's Irish Pub.

Getting There: Metro Transit Route 120 provides service between Downtown and the Burien Transit Center via White Center, stopping near Ambaum Boulevard SW and SW 148th Street. The Eagle Landing trailhead is about 0.9 mile from there one-way: walk along 148th west to Lake Burien Park, then follow the directions from there to the trailhead.

If you're driving, make your way to Burien just west of SeaTac Airport, where westbound SR 518 and SR 509 intersect. Here SR 518 stops, continuing west as SW 148th Street. Stay on 148th until it dead-ends at Lake Burien Park. At this point you have a choice whether to walk or drive the last mile to the trailhead.

From Lake Burien Park, turn left onto 16th Avenue SW, skirting south along the east side of the park. At the next intersection turn right onto SW 149th Street. Three blocks beyond the park, at 22nd Avenue SW, veer slightly right to stay on 149th. After the next intersection, 149th starts curving sharply right. At that point, start looking for the entrance to Eagle Landing Park on the left, just beyond a private driveway. There's a sign, but it's hard to see in advance.

To Eagle Viewing Area: From the trailhead, take the single easy-to-follow trail down and then up and over a small ravine. Soon after the trail tops the ravine, it makes a sharp left curve, and you'll come to a small observation area on the right (1). At this point you're about a quarter of the way to the stairs, a place to pause and look for the Douglas fir that provides a nesting site for the local bald eagle pair. The trail was designed to maintain a 200-foot distance from the eagle tree at all points.

Stepping through the forest canopy

There's a bench where you can settle in for wildlife viewing, and a nice interpretive sign that highlights the main events in the eagle's year: nest-building in January and February; egg-laying in March and April; fledging around July.

As you continue down the trail, you'll pass native plants and trees like vine maple, hazelnut, horsetail, skunk cabbage, Oregon grape, trillium, sword fern, and devil's club. You'll probably also see some of the "dirty dozen" invasive plants that volunteers are working to eradicate. These include the usual suspects that every home gardener knows: English ivy, laurel, bindweed, and foxglove. Volunteers have divided the park into eighteen restoration zones so teams can tackle a zone at a time. Restoring a sustainable native population of plants and trees here is a very doable, if multiyear, project.

To the Eagle Landing Stairs (289 steps): After the eagle-viewing area, the trail moves through a mixed forest of tall conifers and big-leaf maples, with a lush, thriving understory. The terrain is close-in with lots of small humps and hills; the feeling is uniquely intimate and enchanting.

The route passes close to the southern edge of the park, a house barely visible on the left. Then it begins to move generally to the right. You'll make a brief, steep descent before coming to a Y junction, where the trail splits, one fork heading downhill to the left, the other uphill to the right. Take the right fork to

STABLE STAIRS ON A CREEPING HILLSIDE

Here in Eagle Landing Park, water is constantly on the move. It percolates down 5–14 feet of topsoil before encountering a pressure-packed layer of gravelly sand, or till, laid down 14,000 years ago as the last great ice sheet pulled back. This layer is very hard but permeable, so the water continues downward until it reaches a third layer of impermeable clay, the remains of the last glacial lake bottom. At this point the water is forced outward, where it seeps out of the bluff. This creates the small wetlands ecosystem you'll see on either side of the stairs, about 50 feet up from the beach. Gravity also does its thing with the topsoil layer, which creeps imperceptibly toward the beach at up to 0.1 inch per year. The bowed trunks of many trees testify to this movement. All in all, this is a tough spot for stairs.

The stairway that was built here is a special solution to these demanding conditions. The large concrete structures that support the stairs look like massive, steel-reinforced piers buried deep in the hillside, but in reality these "piers" are hollow, and stop at the surface of the topsoil. These are actually "pincaps" from which the real stair supports extend, in the form of strong 2-inch steel pipes, or "pins." The pins reach from the pincaps all the way down through the topsoil, and well into the stable till.

The pincap design meant that construction could be done with hand tools instead of heavy, slope-disturbing equipment. To further spare the slope, portions of stairway were constructed Erector-set fashion off-site, then transported up a temporary, low-impact ramp for final assembly. Another advantage of this design is that topsoil can, to some extent, flow around the pins as it creeps downhill.

the stairs; the left one leads out of sight below, to a locked gate. After walking uphill a bit on the right fork, you'll start descending, and soon you'll see the top of the Eagle Landing stairs (2), with a viewing/resting bench to the left.

You'll find that high-tide storms have eroded the soil and rock at the bottom of the stairs. There is a considerable gap down to the stony beach, and not everyone will feel comfortable making the leap.

The view from the bottom of the stairs reveals a good portion of Vashon Island's eastern shore, from its northern tip down to where Maury Island juts into the Sound. Looking south at that angle you'll also be eyeing Three Tree Point, which extends west into the water from your side of the Sound. Turning to the northwest, it's hard to distinguish the northern tip of Vashon from Blake Island to the right, or Kitsap Peninsula in the background.

Locals tell us that when the tide's out, they often walk over to Seahurst Park along the beach, about 0.5 mile north. If you try it, leave plenty of time to go out and back within the low-tide window: the alternative is a 1.75-mile walk back around, on inland streets. Seahurst Park is a wonderful beach-bound park with a long waterside path and promenade. There's a roomy sheltered picnic area overlooking the beach at the south end, and an environmental science center and marine technology school on the north. There are excellent Puget Sound views everywhere.

Once you've taken in the views here at the bottom, the only way to your starting place is back up the stairs. We recommend checking out the excellent interpretive signs on the way up.

PART IV

EASTSIDE

24 Bellevue: Kelsey Creek Farm

The large tract of forest and wetland in southeast Bellevue is probably *terra incognita* to most people. Luckily, it's easy to explore this historic Eastside location using its excellent stairways, paths, and parklands as a guide. This moderate 1.2-mile route takes place almost entirely within forested park land, along the 10-mile Lake to Lake Trail that connects Lake Sammamish and Lake Washington.

Kelsey Creek Farm Park is 160 acres of farmland, wetland, and hillside forest tucked right inside the city of Bellevue. Two large white barns dominate the western ridge of the park. (WWW) Looking east, your gaze crosses a small valley of meadows and wetlands to rest on the thickly forested, stream-threaded hillside where all the stairway action takes place. The excellent bark-covered trails are springy and easy to navigate, even on rainy days.

Wilburton Hill Park, a few residential blocks northwest, makes a good side trip (see "Option: Side Trip to Wilburton Hill Park and Bellevue Botanical Garden"). Wilburton is 105 acres of second-growth forest that have been incorporated into the Bellevue parks system. It's a generally more open, drier flatland forest than you'll find over at Kelsey Creek Hill, just a few hundred yards away. The real jewel of Wilburton is the 53-acre Bellevue Botanical Garden at the far west end. It costs nothing to explore, and there are beautifully tended footpaths through an alpine rock garden, a native plant garden, and other beautiful display gardens. There's also an extensive loop called the Lost Meadow Trail that might be a good one to come back for.

Length:	**1.2 miles (add 1.9 miles with the side trip to Wilburton Hill Park and Bellevue Botanical Garden)**
Walking Time:	45 minutes (add 1 hour for side trip)
Steps Down:	50
Steps Up:	163

Kid-Friendly: This walk can be drastically shortened by doing just the Kelsey Creek Farm segment. The stairway trail here is short and interesting, and the two huge white barn buildings and farm animals are on view 365 days a year. The historic Fraser Cabin might capture the imagination of the older kids, too. There's a great play area, open grassy parkland, a covered picnic area, and restrooms.

Cafes/Pubs: There are great picnic places at Kelsey Creek Farm Park and Bellevue Botanical Garden.

Getting There: Metro Transit unfortunately doesn't run convenient bus routes to the starting point. By car, take the SE 8th Street exit from I-405, exit number 12 (from either direction), and head east, under the Wilburton Trestle. At the next stoplighted intersection, drive straight ahead. The road immediately curves right, becoming SE 7th Place. Stay on 7th Place as it enters a residential area; when it ends, turn left, onto 130th Place SE. Kelsey Creek Farm will now be visible on your right. When you reach the north end of the park, at SE 4th Place, turn right into the parking area.

To the Kelsey Stairs (163 steps up): Early in the walk you'll see the farm structures off to your right, but the route takes you quickly past them and up into the forested slopes, where you'll find your first stairs. Start from the very north end of the parking lot, walking over the paved bridge (1) that crosses a tributary of Kelsey Creek (Goff Creek). This bridge is one of two good salmon-viewing areas along the trail, with best viewing usually around mid-October.

After you cross the bridge, angle left up a gravel trail to the crown of a small conifer-covered hill. From there, your trail angles left again as it runs downhill to meet another trail that's visible below. Turn left where they meet.

The trail then makes a sharp turn to the right, and soon you'll hear the main body of Kelsey Creek running behind willows to the left. Through the undergrowth you might see the creek, as well as numerous snags that belted kingfishers use as perches from which they fish the creek (watch for birds with a bushy crest, a white collar, and an outsized pointed bill).

At the next junction, turn left onto a bridge that hovers over Kelsey Creek (2), offering a lengthy walkway through the lush wetland. At the far end you'll reach another T junction; head left here (3). You'll pass another trail junction on the right as you make your way toward the first set of timber stairs.

On a landing midway up the stairs, you'll pass another trail heading off to the right. After you've navigated this major stairway and another small flight of just 8 steps, the trail crests into the open as it reaches another T junction. Turn right.

The Pipeline Trail and a Few More Stairs (50 Steps Down): After you turn right at the trail's crest, you'll be heading south along the Pipeline Trail.

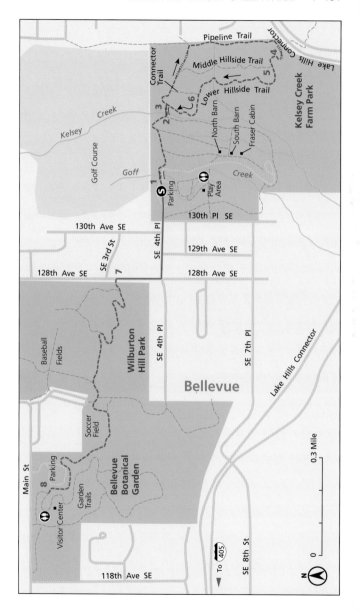

The first Kelsey Creek Farm stairway

There are power lines overhead and houses perched above you to the left of this wide gravel trail. On your right, blackberries and other undergrowth partly conceal the forested slopes you've just emerged from. Almost halfway along you'll pass a white steel barrier protecting a pipeline valve. Olympic Pipe Line Company runs gasoline, diesel, and jet fuel through pipelines between Blaine, Washington and Portland, Oregon—hence the trail's name.

After a few gentle curves and ups-and-downs, the trail dips into a bowl and then back up to approach a roadway on the left, SE 10th Street. Here you'll take the trail to the right, back down into the forest (a sign reads "KELSEY CREEK FARM 0.7 MI.").

As you head down the hillside, you'll encounter the first of several short stairways (4) and small bridges crossing a small stream. At the next signed trail junction, "KELSEY CREEK FARM 0.4 MI.," turn left (5). You'll continue initially downslope (west), but soon the trail turns definitely to the right, heading back north along the length of the hillside. The trail you turned away from at (5) is the "Middle Hillside Trail." It pursues the same course across the hillside, a little higher up.

After crossing a few more rivulets trickling down the hillside, you'll reach another junction (6). Bear left, and soon after that the trail will cross several wooden walkways as it returns to the wetlands of Kelsey Creek. Watch for a low wooden log fence to the left, where you can get an open view of the creek. After this, the trail curves right toward the next junction (3), completing this hillside loop.

At the junction, bear left, reversing your steps over the lengthy Kelsey Creek bridge. Just after you recross the bridge, you have a choice. A right turn at the T junction there (2) will have you retracing your steps, the creek running alongside on your right. A left turn will take you in the direction of the rest of the park, including the stables and historic buildings.

KELSEY CREEK ECOSYSTEM

Kelsey Creek drains a big swath of territory between Lake Sammamish and Lake Washington—almost 11,000 acres in and around the city of Bellevue, even larger than Thornton Creek, Seattle's other major watershed (see walk 5, "Maple Leaf and Thornton Creek"). The horseshoe-shaped creek flows north at first, then traces a wide curve to the west before turning south through Kelsey Creek Farm. From there it flows through Mercer Slough, and then into Lake Washington. Where the creek enters Mercer Slough there's a fish ladder, so salmon and steelhead can make the jump upstream to spawn.

By the early 1900s the land that is now the park had been logged to stumps. Yet today the hillside and adjoining wetlands around this stretch of Kelsey Creek are covered with dense second-growth forest. You'll see Douglas fir and western red cedar as well as towering big-leaf maples and black cottonwoods; a variety of restored native shrubs and plants fills in the lower story. There are lots of standing dead trees, or snags, which make wonderful perches for belted kingfishers in the wetlands, and provide shelter and insect prey for pileated woodpeckers in the hillside forest.

Kelsey Creek Farm Park is great wildlife habitat. We've seen banded pigeons, merlins, brown creepers, spotted towhees, cedar waxwings, red-tailed hawks, and Anna's hummingbirds. The birds come and go with the seasons, as do the salmon. From late September through November, you might spot returning chinook, coho, or sockeye from a couple of Kelsey Creek viewpoints along the trail.

To continue back to your starting place, simply retrace your steps, climbing up and over your initial hill to the parking lot. From there you can take a side trip to Wilburton Hill Park and Bellevue Botanical Garden, which adds 1.9 miles round-trip.

Option: Side Trip to Wilburton Hill Park and Bellevue Botanical Garden

The excursion to Wilburton Hill Park and Bellevue Botanical Garden doesn't have any stairs, but it's well worth the exploration.

From the parking area, walk straight to the exit and onto SE 4th Place, heading west for two blocks. Then turn right onto 128th Avenue SE, walking uphill past a half-dozen houses on your right, until you see the signed trailhead (7) on your left (if you reach SE 3rd Street, you've overshot the trailhead).

Head straight up a broad, gravel trail. After you pass the first side trail on the right, the main trail starts to weave back and forth, headed more or less west. You'll see lots of blackberry bushes, a few huckleberries, and of course lots of trees, but overall the forest is more open than around Kelsey Creek. Watch for an out-of-place boulder sitting off the left side of the trail—a "glacial erratic" dumped here by the last ice sheet as it retreated 14,000 years ago. **WWW**

The main gravel path makes a major turn right (east) before it finally straightens out and heads west in earnest, just where you see a second side trail going off to the right. A few dozen yards beyond, you'll see a couple of baseball backstops to your right and a children's play area, complete with a zip line, ahead. The trail veers left around the play area, then opens out to a luxuriantly artificial turf-covered soccer field. Follow the trail as it parallels the left sideline.

The trail rounds the far end of the soccer field, curving right to head uphill past a small wetland pond below. Soon the trail curves left, skirting Bellevue Botanical Garden's parking lot.

Continue up a sidewalk next to the parking area and up to the Botanical Garden entrance (8). To the right, a ramp winds around an otherwordly entrance garden of tall, slender stacked-rock sculptures standing among colorful grasses. **WWW** There are restrooms inside the airy, light-filled visitor center, a beautiful converted Midcentury residence.

Bellevue Botanical Garden originated with Cal and Harriet Shorts, who built their home here in 1957 and continued to add garden improvements around the property. In 1984 they deeded their home and 7 surrounding acres to the City of Bellevue for use as a park. Subsequent City purchases brought the property to its current 53 acres, a combination of cultivated gardens, restored woodlands, and natural wetlands. More than 300,000

HISTORIC KELSEY CREEK FARM

From the 1880s, the Kelsey Creek Farm lands were owned by a logging company, which harvested all but 5 acres before selling the property in 1921. It was transformed into a dairy operation lasting through World War II. The smaller of the two barns here was built in 1933; the larger barn on the north side was built by a new owner in 1944 as part of an expanded dairy operation. After the war the farm was sold again, and converted to a Hereford beef cattle operation.

South of the two large white barns is historic Fraser Cabin, built several miles away in 1888. Like the farm, the cabin changed hands several times, and it was used variously as a family home, storage shed, and horse barn. When the cabin was moved to Kelsey Creek in 1974, the logs were carefully numbered so it could be accurately reconstructed. A peek inside the cabin brings early days here to life. **WWW**

By the early 1960s, the land around Kelsey Creek Farm was steadily turning into residential developments, and both property values and taxes were rising steeply. When the owners of Kelsey Creek Farm started talking about selling, their neighbors persuaded the City of Bellevue to consider the property as a potential park. In 1968 the owners sold it to the City at a generous price, lower than they would have received from a developer. In turn the City agreed to maintain the property and farm buildings as a park and education center. And that's how a large bucolic park came to sit, improbably, right in Bellevue.

Kelsey Creek Farm Park is a real working farm. The animals can be viewed daily, between the hours of 9:00 AM and 3:30 PM. **WWW** Classes and activities can be found at the park's web page, www.myparksandrecreation.com.

visitors come to Bellevue Botanical Garden annually, with good reason. You can visit theme gardens, take a guided tour, or strike out on your own along a trail system through much of the preserve. There are small waterfalls, ponds, and plants and beautiful flowers of all kinds, carefully labeled and tended by volunteers. There's no charge, except when the garden puts on a spectacular light show each evening through the holidays.

Both the Botanical Garden and Wilburton Hill Park offer more to explore among their extensive trail networks. To return to your starting place, simply retrace your steps back from the garden entrance. ♦

25 Mercer Island: Mercerdale Hillside

Descending Mercerdale Hillside

In 1914, no Seattleite would have bet that Mercer Island would grow to have the largest population of any lake-bound island in the U.S. Back then, without your own boat, the only way to get to this 5-mile-long island was to cross a decaying, little-used wooden bridge from Bellevue, or take the ferry from Leschi in Seattle. The island had lost its main tourist attraction, the gingerbread-palace Calkins

Hotel, to fire in 1908. The Roanoke Inn, still in business, was a popular hangout close to the ferry landing, but there wasn't much else happening in isolated "East Seattle."

Jump ahead to 1940, when the new floating bridge opened the floodgates to rapid growth. Twenty years later, the City of Mercer Island incorporated, and preservation of some remaining open space suddenly became a City imperative. In 1964 the City acquired 113 acres on the south side of the island, which became the wonderful forested trail system called Pioneer Park. Many other open spaces were purchased, about 300 acres in all.

This stairway walk takes place mostly in 19-acre Mercerdale Hillside, which abuts 12-acre Mercerdale Park, at the base of Mercerdale Hillside. Both sites are managed by the Mercer Island Parks and Recreation Department. A magnificent system of paths and stairways, developed in 1981, provides access to some of the most beautiful and charming greenspace on the island. Mercer Island is shaped something like a giant right footprint, heel toward the southern end of Lake Washington. The route is at the base of the big toe, close to the oldest settled areas of the island.

The walk has two major sections, each with its distinctive pleasures and, of course, stairways. The first part takes you along a beautiful, meandering timber stairway from the top of the picturesque hillside to the bottom. Along the way you'll pass several side paths that disappear into the forested slope, whetting your appetite for the second part of the walk: a stroll along the hillside itself. After skirting the bottom of the hillside, you'll reenter the trail system to explore the Douglas fir forest at the south end, perhaps with an eagle sighting. After a short detour through the neighborhood above, you'll head back north along the length of the hillside, watching as the trees change from conifer to deciduous and back again.

Length:	**2 miles**
Walking Time:	1 hour
Steps Down:	522
Steps Up:	329
Kid-Friendly:	Mercerdale Park (below Mercerdale Hillside's north end) has restrooms and a nifty play area at the bottom of the initial, 321-step downhill stairway. If the climb back up sounds daunting, you can park right at Mercerdale Park, near SE 32nd Street and 78th Avenue SE. From there, you can use it as home base for ad-lib excursions onto the hillside paths and stairs.
Cafes/Pubs:	You'll find eateries a short walk north from Mercerdale Park. Roanoke Inn is a great stop after this walk (see "Option: Side Trip to Roanoke Landing").

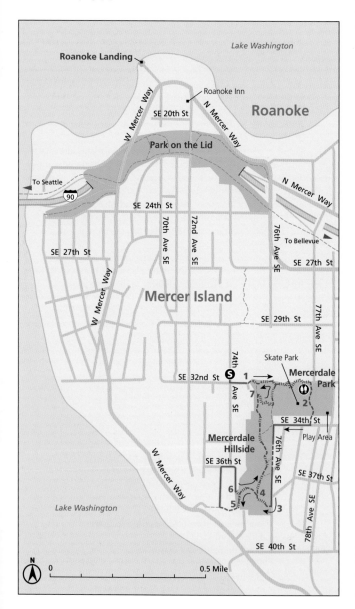

Getting There: If you're driving from Seattle, take exit 6, W Mercer Way, off the eastbound I-90 floating bridge. Turn right at the end of the off-ramp and then one block later turn left, heading east on SE 24th Street. After five blocks turn right onto 72nd Avenue SE and drive 0.5 mile south, then turn left onto SE 32nd Street. Park near the northeast corner of 32nd and 74th Avenue SE.

If you're taking the bus, Metro Transit Routes 201 and 204 from Downtown stop near the post office just northeast of Mercerdale Park. From there you can join the walk midway through (see "Mercerdale Park to the Mercerdale Hillside Trail").

SE 32nd Street Stairs (321 steps down): From SE 32nd and 74th Avenue SE, walk east along 32nd to the top of the stairs (1). This spectacular timber stairway weaves all the way down the northern portion of the Mercerdale Hillside. At the top, houses approach the stairway along its northern edge, but to the south there's nothing but forested hillside all the way down. The stairway has an unusual two-lane design: a protective handrail runs along one edge, but the handrail on the other side is inset about a third of the way in. This means that if you're a lone walker, you have your own lane if several people, or a person and a dog, are approaching from the other direction.

On the way to the bottom of the hillside, you'll pass three junctions. The first of these clearly runs off into the forest on your right. Just after that first junction, your path turns slightly to the right as it continues generally down the hill.

At the second junction, it's the left arm you'll want to avoid. It curves north down some stairs and quickly reaches a paved lane.

The third junction is a bit trickier. Approaching it, you'll initially find yourself angling to the right, into the hillside. At the junction, take the left branch in order to stay on the main route downhill; the right branch heads across the hillside.

At the bottom you'll step into a small sunken plaza (Bicentennial Park), with the open expanse of Mercerdale Park ahead to the right. There's a restroom directly to the right of Bicentennial Park.

Mercerdale Park to the Mercerdale Hillside Trail (34 steps up): From the plaza area, enter Mercerdale Park and find the perimeter sidewalk around the west side. You'll walk past a native plant garden and then a skate park, both on the right. The native plant garden (2) is a nifty little space with peaceful trails. Across from the skate park you'll see the play area, which has one section devoted to toddlers.

After the skate park, the sidewalk curves gently to the left and then straightens as it approaches the south exit. As you leave Mercerdale Park, turn right to ascend steeply rising SE 34th Street. Then turn left onto 76th Avenue SE, continuing past a tempting stairway up into the forested hillside on your right.

After you pass three houses on the left, the street ends and a footpath temporarily replaces it. You'll pass yet another stairway that disappears up into the hillside, and then 76th Place SE comes in from the left to put you back on pavement. Just after that, you'll pass a third stairway heading up into the hillside. SE 37th Place merges from the left, and then you'll see your path curving into the Mercerdale Hillside woods, marked by wooden bollards at the entrance (3).

You've entered the southern end of the Mercerdale Hillside trail network. You'll meander a bit at this end, exploring the Douglas fir forest and the adjacent neighborhood, before heading back north along the Mercerdale Hillside Trail.

Your path curves immediately to the right, passing through a section of heavily replanted forest. Then you'll march up 34 timber stairs before reaching a trail junction (4). Take the trail to the left; the right-hand trail is your eventual return path.

To the Eagle's Domain (29 steps up, 24 steps down): Heading west from the junction, you'll climb another 24 timber steps. At the top you'll see a stairway coming down to your trail from the right (the return of the loop you're

Heading north along Mercerdale Hillside

about to make). Keep left (south) on the path, dropping down 11 steps and then up 5. At the top of the latter stairs, there's a tree just off the left side of the trail (5); from here you can search the woods to the east for an eagle's nest, high up one of the nearby Douglas fir trees. If you're lucky, an early-summer visit might be rewarded with the sights and sounds of eagle parents feeding their brood. After 13 timber steps down, the trail comes to an end, right across from a house and a residential lane that comes in from the right. Head up the lane.

A Quick Turn through the Neighborhood (43 steps down): You've now embarked on a brief foray outside Mercerdale Hillside Park. Take a look at the second residence on the left, an interesting Japanese-style structure. It features an elaborate garden and teahouse, protected from prying eyes by traditional walls.

At the next street, turn right onto 73rd Avenue SE, a residential street with conifers scattered here and there among the homes. Continue for a long block, then turn right onto SE 36th Street, walking east.

After one block continue past 74th Avenue SE on the left, and past a "DEAD END" sign marking the street ahead. As advertised, the street soon ends at a couple of driveways. Turn right to follow the only street remaining, walking south a short distance before it, too, ends. Straight ahead you'll encounter a driveway on the right and a narrow asphalt path on the left, the two separated by a hedge.

Take the asphalt path to the left. Skirting alongside the hedge, you'll suddenly come to the top of a stairway (6). Take these 38 stairs down, followed by a short section of path and another 5 timber steps to the next junction, turning left to rejoin the same path you came up, but this time heading east.

Across the Hillside (85 steps up, 24 steps down): After heading down the 24 timber steps you ascended earlier, the trail returns to the first junction with the main Mercerdale Hillside Trail (4). At this point turn left on the Hillside Trail. You're now returning north, through the length of Mercerdale Hillside Park. You'll pass three paths coming in from the right, the same paths you'd noticed heading up into the hillside from the bottom. As you progress along the trail, enjoy the changing nature of the vegetation. You'll pass from mostly conifers at the south end to deciduous forest and back again.

Keep count of the junctions, because that's how you'll know where to turn next. The first junction is preceded by 14 steps down; the second by 10 steps down; the third junction is preceded by a long, curving section of 26 steps up.

After the third junction you'll walk your longest stretch before arriving at a fourth junction, which is slightly tricky to find. Keep an eye out for a rise to the right of the trail that has a stairway handrail peeking up over the other side (7).

The Final Leg (181 steps up, 110 steps down): From this junction the main route turns right, up the small rise. You can continue straight ahead too, and either way you'll reach the first stairway of the walk (1), which you'll take back up to your starting place. The route described here is a scenic stretch on a spur trail that's well worth taking.

After you turn right, you'll step down 110 steps to the next junction. At the bottom, the trail turns south, which makes it easy to miss this junction and the trail that heads to the north. The north trail is what you want to take, so turn sharply left and head toward the next stairway, which is visible ahead.

The stairway goes up 48 steps. At the top you'll reach a T intersection at your initial set of stairs. Return from here up a final 133 steps to your starting place.

Option: Side Trip to Roanoke Ferry Landing and Roanoke Inn

The "East Seattle" post office opened on the island in 1904, but in 1924 the rural settlement's name was changed to Mercer Island, in honor of Thomas Mercer, an early Seattle pioneer who suggested the names of Lake Washington and Lake Union. By this time there was active ferry service, mainly to the Roanoke Ferry Landing. The dock structures for the landing are long gone, but a narrow strip of street-end marks the site, now a public park. The views across the lake can be magnificent. **WWW**

A visit to nearby Roanoke Inn (1914) gives additional local and historical flavor. **WWW** It's said to be the oldest business on the island, having started out as a chicken-dinner restaurant and variously served as hotel, brothel, and speakeasy. The interior is dark and comfy, there's a front patio with dining, and the backyard patio has lake views. The Roanoke Inn is a favorite hangout for locals and bicyclists from across the bridge.

To get to Roanoke Landing from your starting/ending place, drive west on SE 32nd Street. Turn right (north) onto 72nd Avenue SE, then drive 0.5 mile to SE 24th Street and turn left. Drive 0.2 mile to W Mercer Way and turn right. Drive 0.4 mile north to Roanoke Way and turn left (W Mercer Way begins a sharp rightward curve at this point). The landing is at the end of the street/driveway.

To reach the Roanoke Inn from the landing, return to W Mercer Way and turn left, continuing in the same direction as before you turned onto Roanoke Way. As W Mercer Way passes Roanoke Way and begins its sharp curve, it becomes SE 22nd Street and heads east for a block. Then it curves again to the right and heads south as it passes N Mercer Way, which forks off to the left. Keep going straight, and Roanoke Inn comes up quickly on the right. ♦

INDEX

ABOUT THE AUTHORS

Jake and Cathy Jaramillo's inspiration for this book goes back to many happy hours walking the stairways of Los Angeles with Cathy's parents, following the classic *Stairway Walks in Los Angeles* by Adah Bakalinsky and Larry Gordon. Jake and Cathy are enthusiastic Seattle transplants, having moved to the Pacific Northwest from Southern California a dozen years ago. Nosing around, they were overjoyed to discover many stairway trails through diverse and colorful

neighborhoods but disappointed that Seattle had no guidebook for exploring some of the best of them (unlike other stairway-rich cities like Pittsburgh, Berkeley, San Francisco, and Portland, Oregon). When they're not tramping around town, Jake and Cathy love to hike local mountain trails, car-camp, and bicycle the growing rails-to-trails network around the country. Jake volunteers as a backpack trip leader with Sierra Club National Outings. Cathy is a former president of the Seattle Audubon Society and continues to volunteer on behalf of birds and nature.
www.seattlestairwaywalks.com

THE MOUNTAINEERS, founded in 1906, is a nonprofit outdoor activity and conservation organization whose mission is "to explore, study, preserve, and enjoy the natural beauty of the outdoors ... " Based in Seattle, Washington, it is now one of the largest such organizations in the United States, with seven branches throughout Washington State.

The Mountaineers sponsors both classes and year-round outdoor activities in the Pacific Northwest, which include hiking, mountain climbing, ski-touring, snowshoeing, bicycling, camping, canoeing and kayaking, nature study, sailing, and adventure travel. The Mountaineers' conservation division supports environmental causes through educational activities, sponsoring legislation, and presenting informational programs.

All activities are led by skilled, experienced volunteers, who are dedicated to promoting safe and responsible enjoyment and preservation of the outdoors.

If you would like to participate in these organized outdoor activities or programs, consider a membership in The Mountaineers. For information and an application, write or call The Mountaineers Program Center, 7700 Sand Point Way NE, Seattle, WA 98115-3996; phone 206-521-6001; visit www.mountaineers.org; or email info@mountaineers.org.

The Mountaineers Books, an active, nonprofit publishing program of The Mountaineers, produces guidebooks, instructional texts, historical works, natural history guides, and works on environmental conservation. All books produced by The Mountaineers Books fulfill the mission of The Mountaineers. Visit www.mountaineersbooks.org to find details about all our titles and the latest author events, as well as videos, web clips, links, and more!

The Mountaineers Books
1001 SW Klickitat Way, Suite 201
Seattle, WA 98134
800-553-4453
mbooks@mountaineersbooks.org

The Mountaineers Books is proud to be a corporate sponsor of The Leave No Trace Center for Outdoor Ethics, whose mission is to promote and inspire responsible outdoor recreation through education, research, and partnerships. The Leave No Trace program is focused specifically on human-powered (nonmotorized) recreation.

Leave No Trace strives to educate visitors about the nature of their recreational impacts and offers techniques to prevent and minimize such impacts. Leave No Trace is best understood as an educational and ethical program, not as a set of rules and regulations.

For more information, visit www.lnt.org, or call 800-332-4100.

OTHER TITLES YOU MIGHT ENJOY FROM
THE MOUNTAINEERS BOOKS

**Winter Hikes of Western Washington Deck:
The 50 Best (Mostly) Snow-Free Trails**
Craig Romano
A smart and portable way to hit
the trails all year long

Nature in the City: Seattle
Kathryn True and Maria Dolan
The best walks to see eagles, seals,
flower gardens, and other
wild gems without leaving town

**The Healthy Back Book: A Guide to Whole
Healing for Outdoor Enthusiasts and Other
Active People**
Dr. Astrid Pujari and Nancy Schatz Alton
Accessible advice and simple exercises to ease
lower back pain and
discomfort

**The Healthy Knees Book: A Guide to
Whole Healing for Outdoor Enthusiasts
and Other Active People**
Dr. Astrid Pujari and Nancy Schatz Alton
Accessible advice to make recovery from
knee pain or injury easier to achieve

**The Zen of Wilderness and Walking:
Wit, Wisdom, and Inspiration**
Foreword by Bill McKibben
From Chinese proverbs to bumper stickers,
this is a thought-provoking yet whimsical
collection of quotes about why we walk
in the woods

**The Mountaineers Books has more than
500 outdoor recreation titles in print.**
For more details visit
www.mountaineersbooks.org.